That's Why We're Here

That's Why We're Here

STORIES FROM PASSIONATE JAMES TAYLOR FANS

REBECCA LYN GOLD

For information about this title or to order other books and/or electronic media, contact the publisher:

LWJT Press

LifeWithJamesTaylor.com

info@LifeWithJamesTaylor.com

ISBN: 978-1-7361805-0-1 (print)
         978-1-7361805-1-8 (ebook)

Printed in the United States of America

Cover photo: Osvaldo Gold
Author photo: Pamela Sardinha

Cover and Interior design: 1106 Design

CONTENTS

INTRODUCTION

The most remarkable thing about James Taylor's music is its ability to spark connection. We connect with James, we connect with ourselves, and we connect with each other. His music, his stories, and that beautiful, velvety voice makes us feel like we are not alone.

My personal connection with James Taylor's music began when I was 13 years old, going through a very lonely and traumatic period in my life. One day, when my music teacher played the song "Fire And Rain," I instantly felt a connection—like James was singing TO ME. All the pain, the abandonment, the loneliness, the sadness … all of it was right there in that song, and I felt like I wasn't alone anymore. Someone *got* me. He knew the pain I knew, he felt the abandonment I felt, he sang to me and he told me through his story that it would all be OK. He gave me hope.

The story doesn't end there. And neither does James Taylor's relevance and inspiration in my life. He continued through the next four decades to write and sing songs that touched me deeply throughout different periods, difficult as well as glorious moments.

I can't tell you how many James Taylor concerts I've been to. Literally, I can't. From the early 1970s to the present day, as soon as a tour is announced, tickets are in my hand. And every time I see him walk on stage and nod to the crowd, an overwhelming feeling of love and gratitude fills my heart, and I silently thank him, once again, for saving my life.

One of the best things that happens at a JT concert is the instant connection his fans have with each other. Regardless of who is standing next to me, we immediately bond and share our JT love stories. I'm a sucker for a good JT story; I want to hear them all!

So, a few years ago, I created the Facebook page *Life With James Taylor*. My vision was to create a space to be able to connect with others who, like me, share a passion for the music of James Taylor. The stories that have been shared both on the page and in private messages to me have been amazing. I laugh, I cry, and half the time I think "that's me, too!" Ultimately, I decided I didn't want to keep the stories to myself. I want to share them with those I refer to as my JTBFFs!

And that is how this book project – ***That's Why We're Here: Stories from Passionate James Taylor Fans*** – began.

Thank you to all my JTBFFs who shared their stories with me and each other. I wish I could include them all, but I've had to narrow it down to what can fit in this one volume. I hope to continue to share stories with my JTBFFs on my Facebook page and in concert venues around the world. Because, as you know, *that's why we're here!*

CHAPTER 1

My Story

Rebecca Lyn Gold

Mrs. Almeda was pretty cool, kind of a hippy, but not really. She had long black hair with gray streaks, and it was always messy, like she'd just crawled out of bed. She dressed in bright colored maxi skirts with peasant blouses and a wide belt cinched at the waist. She wore long dangly earrings and a bunch of bracelets on both wrists that jingled when she walked. She played the guitar and the piano and had a pretty good singing voice, too. I liked her, even though I thought she was too old to dress the way she did. And I liked her music class, especially when she brought in records of new singers she wanted us to listen to. We would talk about the lyrics or the melody and why we liked or didn't like the song. I never said much in class, but I liked listening to the music, and she never made us sit at our desks if we didn't want to, so I usually stood in the back of the room where I could remain unnoticed.

"OK kids, settle down," she said as she flowed into the room, her guitar strapped around her embroidered blouse. "I want to introduce you to one of my favorite singers. Listen carefully, and then we'll talk about the song."

She propped up the album cover in front of the record player, then carefully placed the needle of the turntable on the record, lifting it a few times to get it to just the right spot. A guitar intro began, and she turned the volume up high. With her long black hair swinging back and forth, she started to sing softly along with the record.

That day, most of the kids in class were talking to each other and not paying much attention, but there was something about the singer's voice that drew me in, so I walked closer to the front of the classroom to hear the lyrics more clearly.

Mrs. Almeda was singing along quietly and strumming her guitar, with her eyes closed.

"I've seen fire and I've seen rain…"

I closed my eyes, too, and listened.

The last line hit me. I literally felt like someone had punched me in the chest, and I couldn't breathe. I sat down in one of the desks, as close as I could get to the record player, and listened more closely, as the song continued.

This singer, with the most beautiful voice I had ever heard, was singing exactly what I was feeling. My body ached in the exact way his words described. And I, too, felt like I wasn't going to make it to the other side of the darkness I was in.

I started to cry. First, just a little sob. And then, as Mrs. Almeda belted out the chorus, something inside of me burst wide open. Everything that I had been feeling – abandonment, confusion, fear, sadness, loneliness – all of it had been captured in that one song.

I opened my eyes and saw Mrs. Almeda looking right at me. I was so embarrassed, realizing that I had been crying out loud.

"Are you OK, Becky?" she asked.

I got up and walked as fast as I could out of the room to the bathroom down the hall. I couldn't stop the tears from pouring out of me. I was sobbing uncontrollably, and I didn't know how to make it stop. Alone in the bathroom stall, I just cried and cried and cried.

What Mrs. Almeda didn't know, nor did anyone else at the time, was that within the timespan of one year, everything I knew to be true had been turned upside down. After eighteen years, my parents' traditional Greek marriage had fallen apart. My father moved out and left my mother with four children to fend for ourselves. We lost our five-bedroom suburban home with a big backyard on a cul-de-sac and moved to a two-bedroom apartment in a nearby city. My mother worked multiple jobs as a waitress and bartender to make ends meet and was experiencing freedom for the first time in her life, which left my siblings and me on our own much of the time. My older sister, who was my best friend, moved in with my grandmother, who was dying of lung cancer. And to top it off, I had found my way into the home of an older man who was posing as a guitar teacher, but, as I later learned, was a leader in the Adidam cult.

He lured teenagers like me into his home, kids who were vulnerable and lost—latchkey kids. Through drugs, mind games, sex and secrets, he seduced and manipulated us into thinking that we could be happy if we were devotees of his group, and that what he was doing was good for us: providing a family that we lacked and needed.

So while my own close-knit Greek family was falling apart, this leader of the Adidam cult was offering a way for me to be part of a family again. And every week as I went for my guitar lessons (which were nothing of the sort), I got sucked in further, and it was confusing and dangerous. I was scared and lonely and had no one to turn to. I even considered suicide.

Until this singer, this stranger, sang a song that rattled my inner being. I felt his pain, his struggles, and this made me feel like I wasn't alone anymore. He brought me into his world through his songs and gave me the strength and the words to finally break open the truth about what was going on behind closed doors in my guitar teacher's home.

In the midst of my trauma, I did not have the words to express what was happening. I could not make sense of the experiences or my desire to continue to be a part of it. Something inside my brain broke open that day, when I heard James Taylor sing about his own pain and suffering. His voice, his words, allowed me to find the language for my own healing to begin.

I went directly to the neighborhood record store and listened to every James Taylor album they had. The store manager saw how distraught I was and allowed me to "borrow" the *Sweet Baby James* album, because I didn't have the money to buy it. That night, I listened to every song on that album over and over. "Blossom," "Anywhere Like Heaven," and of course, "Fire And Rain." They inspired me to open my journal and write down everything I was feeling, everything going on in my guitar teacher's home. The drugs, the sex, the manipulation, the mind games, all of it. When I went to bed that night, I left my journal open in my mother's bedroom in the hope that she would read it when she got home from work. She did; and so began the journey for me to get the help I needed. I never went back to the Adidam group after that day.

The story doesn't end there. In fact, it is where it begins. James Taylor's relevance and inspiration in my life has continued through

the next four decades. He has continued to write and sing songs that have touched me deeply throughout different periods of my life. And I continue to take the *breadcrumbs* of his music and inspiration to follow a path to my own true and healed self, through episodes of PTSD, depression, divorce, struggles with infertility, as well as through glorious moments: the birth and adoption of my children, living in South America, marrying my soulmate.

In her memoir, *My Story*, Elizabeth Smart writes about her own coping mechanisms after she was freed from nine months of captivity. She says that "Music is the unspoken language that can convey feelings more accurately than talking ever could." For Elizabeth Smart, playing the harp was her therapy and meditation. For me, it was the music of James Taylor.

I did not know any of this when, at 13 years old, I was drawn into the music of James Taylor. I did not know that my own healing would come through his music and continue to be a defining force in my life.

Today, at 60 years old and more than 60 concerts later, all that is left to say is: *Thank You, James.*

That's why I'm here.

CHAPTER 2

Another Grey Morning

Dave Zwayer – Toledo, OH

I am the oldest of five children; we are each one year apart in age. My parents got divorced when I was 11 years old, and I ended up living with my father, stepmother, and my two youngest siblings.

In 1976, I was a very lonely, lost, depressed, and confused 15-year-old boy. One of the ways I found to help cope with life at that time was music. I must have joined Columbia House Record Club five times under different pseudonyms (including all of my siblings' names!).

While browsing through LP selections I happened upon the cover of *JT* and thought, "He looks like a nice guy, I wonder how his music is." So, having to order my "11 albums for a penny," I chose the *JT* album. And I'm glad I did.

From the first note of "Your Smiling Face" I thought I was onto something, but it wasn't until I heard him sing the song "Another Grey Morning" that I KNEW I had to hear everything this guy had ever recorded. Not sure why, not sure how, and I knew he was singing about a girl/woman, but for whatever reason that song spoke volumes to me. I can't really even put into words how it made me feel, except to say that song, perhaps, saved my life.

It's hard to describe. It's as if his songs and I were on the same "wavelength," if that makes sense. After hearing everything else James recorded, I can tell you what each and every song means to me.

I am now a member of the local stagehands in Toledo, Ohio. Because of this, I've met quite a few artists. But I can tell you, there are none like James Taylor.

On February 26, 2019, James came to perform in Toledo. I helped set up the stage with his roadies. Before the show, I came early on the off chance I could meet (and maybe get a picture with) my musical idol. As it happened, I was walking out of catering as he was walking in.

I approached him and said, "Hello Mr. Taylor. I want to tell you I'm one of your biggest fans. I've seen you twenty-two times in concert, the last being at Wrigley Field with Jackson Browne. I have multiple copies of every album you've done, including all in your discography, which are still sealed, and I actually just purchased your new pop-up book for my 2-year-old granddaughter, Penelope."

He shook my hand and said, "Would you like me to sign it for her?"

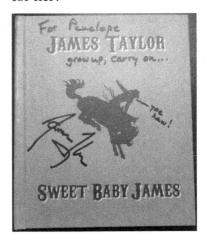

Somewhat taken off guard, I replied, "Well, I don't have it with me, but I was hoping to get a picture with you to put in the book for her."

Without hesitation he said, "Of course," and put his arm around me for the picture. While I was shaking his hand and thanking him, he looked at me with a wry smile and said, "Wait right here, I think I may have another one of those books." He came back a few minutes later with his book. As we sat down together, he removed it from the sealed package and proceeded to autograph the book cover with her name and a message.

As we sat there, I told him about the songs and albums that really drew me to him, "Another Grey Morning" from the album *JT*, was high on the list. He told me that song was mostly about his mother.

Needless to say, I was overwhelmed by his kindness and generosity and got a bit choked up. It is a day I'll never forget. This man is even nicer than everyone thinks he is.

Anyway, that's my story, and I'm sticking to it.

Thank you, James.

CHAPTER 3

Anywhere Like Heaven

Fran Mulvihill – Pottstown, PA

In 1965, at the age of 44, my mother was diagnosed with breast cancer. Five years later, on September 21, 1970, we said our goodbyes. I was 16 years old.

I was lost, lonely, and so sad for months afterward. In December of the same year, I went into a record store with five dollars in my pocket, just to look around. I saw the cover of *Sweet Baby James*, and thought, "That boy is cute." And although I had never heard of James Taylor, I bought the album, simply because I liked the cover.

I took it home and fell in love. James Taylor had the most soothing voice I had ever heard. The song "Anywhere Like Heaven" spoke to me, especially the first line. I had a fascination with New York City back then (still do); that song took me there, and reminded me to get out there and live!

I can't explain it, but I feel like that *Sweet Baby James* album saved my life. It made me feel like everything was going to be OK; that I was going to be OK; and I was.

I still feel the same way, fifty years later. James Taylor has always been there for me.

CHAPTER 4

Blossom

Kelly Wissler – Nashville, TN

When I was 25 years old, I was going through a really rough time. My panic and anxiety were at an all-time high. Nothing could stop the spiral once a panic attack began. I was missing work. My "magic pill" wasn't working anymore. In fact, I was taking more than twice the prescribed dosage just to keep from going into withdrawal.

I made an appointment with a therapist in hopes that she could help with the panic and anxiety that was taking all the joy from my life. We didn't make it past my list of medications before she recommended that I check myself into a drug rehab program. What? I'm not a drug addict; it's all prescribed by a doctor! On the drive home I tried to convince myself that this doctor didn't know what she was talking about … I'd just go see someone else.

But she had been right. I had my mom drive me to rehab and checked myself in. When they searched my bag, they took my Walkman, but let me know they had some others available, along with relaxation tapes. They didn't take the tapes I had brought with me, all James Taylor.

Needless to say, when they took away my downers, I was unable to sleep. I asked for the Walkman and put in James. After all, he had gone through this too … he had my back … he'd see me through. I would get my strength and my serenity through his music and our shared experience. When the worst of the withdrawal symptoms hit, bringing on major panic, his music was the only thing that would calm me down. "Blossom" was my go-to.

Thirty plus years later, I'm still clean and sober. I have healthy ways to deal with panic and anxiety, and I'm living my best life every day. James Taylor saved my life. I don't know that I would have stuck it out without his music.

I attend concerts alone … my time with James. A couple of years ago I was finally able to snag an autograph! Not easy for someone prone to panic attacks to stand in that crowd.

Thank you is not enough.

Thank you, James.

∽

Janine Johnson – Downers Grove, IL

I am a lifelong fan of James Taylor and have loved every song he has written and performed. When I first heard "Blossom" on the *Sweet Baby James* album, I was moved and inspired to create a piece of artwork in his honor: a small stained-glass window decorated with blossoming irises, my favorite flower.

The year was 1980. It was winter, and my friend and I had tickets to James' concert at the Holiday Star Theatre in Merrillville, Indiana. I packed the stained-glass window, along with a note thanking James for all the enjoyment he had given me over the years. With my parcel in hand, my friend and I drove through blizzard conditions to get to the concert. I was concerned that we'd never make it there in time, but luckily, we did!

Because security was not as tight then as it is today, I was able to carry my small package into the venue. During the second half of the concert, I approached the stage, unwrapped my gift, and set it down on the stage. When James finished his concert, he came to the edge of the stage to gather the flowers that several fans had put there for him. As the spotlights moved, the lights reflected off my window. That caught James' eye. He walked across the stage, picked up my gift, and walked backstage with my gift in his hands. I was overjoyed, knowing that I was able to give something back to James, who had given so much to me through the years.

I am a retired art teacher, and during my thirty-five years of teaching, I often played JT's music in my classroom, hoping to inspire my students to *blossom* while passing James' music on to the next generation.

CHAPTER 5

Carolina In My Mind

Maria Economou – New Milford, CT

I have attended a James Taylor concert almost every year for the past fifteen years. Of all my concert experiences, two stand out above the rest.

First, my girlfriend and I saw James at Madison Square Garden about ten years ago. Miraculously, we had gotten tenth row center seats. To this day, we don't know how that happened. As the concert progressed, we couldn't wait until James sang our favorite, "Carolina In My Mind." In unison, we yelled out, "James! Please sing 'Carolina!'" Suddenly, James looked up at us, picked up the chalkboard with the set list on it, pointed, and said, "Patience, girls! Look—here is where we are, and here is 'Carolina.'" Then he smiled his amazing smile. Four songs later, as he began to sing "Carolina In My Mind," he said, "This one is for you girls." It was a magical moment.

Five years later, we saw James at Mohegan Sun in Connecticut. This time, we were so far back that anyone could have been up there singing and we wouldn't have known the difference. But the acoustics were great, so we really enjoyed it regardless.

At intermission, I noticed that James was not leaving the stage with his band; instead he moved toward the front and sat down at the edge. I immediately grabbed my girlfriend's hand and dragged her with me toward the stage. We ran past the guard so quickly that he never got a chance to stop us. Suddenly, the crowd also noticed what was happening and people began to swarm around us. We were being pushed closer and closer to the stage. In a minute, we arrived virtually up against James' knees. I looked up at him, inches away, and said, "May I have your autograph, Master?"

He said, "Master? Sure!"

I was mortified, but I cherished my first autograph!

Recently on YouTube I watched and heard James sing "You Can Close Your Eyes" with Kim and Henry Taylor. I actually cried when he looked at Kim while he sang, "I still love you," and at Henry when he sang, "You can sing this when I'm gone."

James Taylor has brought so much joy to my life and to others. Bless him always.

❧

Pat Evans - Philippi, WV

When I was a teenager and started to cultivate my own taste in music, James Taylor caught my attention. I fell in love with his smooth voice and gentle singing; he was my favorite artist to listen to. When I realized he also played the guitar, I wanted to sing and play just like him.

In 1967, when I was about 17, I bought two of his albums, including his *Greatest Hits*, and the songbook that went with it. I purchased a cheap guitar and taught myself to play by learning the song "Carolina In My Mind." I was absolutely in love with that song! I learned to play his other songs too, like "You've Got A Friend" and "Fire And Rain."

In 1971, when I was 21 and living in Pittsburgh, I saw him and Carole King in concert for the first time. Seeing two of my favorite artists onstage felt like a miracle. The memory of that night will forever be etched in my heart.

Another great memory I have of James was seeing him at the Ritz Carlton in NYC in 2004. I was visiting the city with a friend and saw a man with a guitar, tall and thin, with a "golf-like" hat, just the type of hat JT wears, walk out of the hotel with his back to us. I knew it was James Taylor. I was too shocked and shy to yell, "Hey, James!" but to this day, I wish I would have. To have a selfie with my favorite singer in the world is the only thing on my bucket list.

I have a band now in our small town of Philippi, West Virginia. We sing duets of "It's Too Late" and "Mockingbird." I also sing "Carolina In My Mind." When we are sitting around in our living rooms, we always come up different JT songs to sing. When I listen to James play, I get lost in his voice and how easy the words flow. He absolutely sings from the heart, and I find myself right there with him.

If I was stranded on a deserted island and could only have one album with me, it would have to be *James Taylor's Greatest Hits*, 1976. I guess you'd say I am a lifelong, HUGE James Taylor fan.

Thank You, James.

❧

Les Sperling - Lake Worth, FL

My wife Michelle, whom I met in 1971 when I was 16 years old, first introduced me to James Taylor's music. She almost exclusively played James Taylor and Carly Simon. Listening to music together was always special for us; I can still remember her face as she sang along to James' music, dancing easily to the melody.

In 1995, Michelle was diagnosed with Alzheimer's. When she was close to dying, we played James' music to comfort her. She passed away in 2016, but James' voice sends me back to those times we sat side by side, swaying to the music we both loved.

"Carolina In My Mind" still brings tears to my eyes. Although it sometimes breaks my heart, I will never stop listening to the music that brings memories of Michelle flooding back to me.

❧

Jen Sperling (Les' daughter)

The first time I heard James Taylor was when I was a teenager and my mom sent me an e-card. That was just the kind of person she was. We would send cards back and forth sometimes with different sayings about friendship, mother/daughter love, that kind of a thing. "You've Got A Friend" was the song that played when the card opened. It was only the instrumental version, but it pushed me to seek out the song. When I heard James Taylor sing it, I was immediately hooked.

My mom was my best friend and a James Taylor fan for as long as I can remember. We never got a chance to see James live, but we loved sitting together and listening to his music.

"You've Got A Friend" has been a special song for my mom and me in a lot of ways. When she was diagnosed with early-onset Alzheimer's, I would play her favorite music as a way for us to stay connected. James Taylor was always on the playlist. A few days before she passed away, my sister and I sat by her bedside and played "You've Got A Friend." She was in a comatose state, but the doctors said she could still hear us. I believe in my heart that she heard that song and knew we were with her in the end.

She passed away in January of 2016 at the young age of 60, and while I am obviously devastated, hearing his music now makes me miss my mom and feel comforted at the same time. His music soothes me. I hope someday I'll get a chance to see him in concert; I know my mom will be right there with me, in spirit, singing away.

CHAPTER 6

Copperline

Nancy Dimit Anderson – Indianapolis, IN

I have loved James Taylor's voice and music since I was 16 years old. I'm currently 66. There is a James Taylor song for just about every special occasion in my life. I have three children, and there's a song that goes with each one of them. My oldest daughter, Jaymi's (named for James) song is "Your Smiling Face." My youngest daughter, Paige, is my "hippie traveler." Her song is "Carolina In My Mind."

My son Andy's song is "Something In The Way She Moves." I know this is an odd choice for a SON, but that is the beauty of James' songs; we find our own meaning in the lyrics, even if it is vastly different from what James had written about.

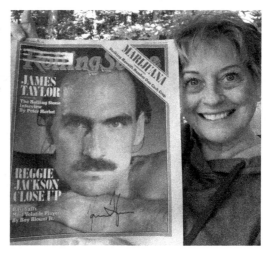

Andy was having a horrible time during his

college years with panic, anxiety and agoraphobia. He came home from the university out of fear that his life was coming to an end, and basically confined himself to his bed for months. He seemed to think at that time that I (his mom) was the only one that could save him. So I stayed by him, sitting next to his bed, holding his hand during the roughest times, just talking to him, reading the Bible, trying to entertain his mind, for hours, days, weeks on end.

I listened to James' song "Something In The Way She Moves" over and over again. For me, the song tells the story of a mom helping her son through mental anxiety robbing him of life, happiness, and everything he had known. That song reminded me that it wasn't what I had to say, or the meaning behind my words, but rather just the sound of the words repeated with love that could calm him down. Day by day, Andy got better. He helped himself to get better; I was just there to be a support, provide a distraction, help him gain strength, endure the mental anxiety and agoraphobia and help him avoid the places in his mind that were too scary to go to.

After Andy got strong enough to be on his own again, sometimes he would need to call me to calm him down if the anxiety came back. Any time of the day or night, I would stop and do my best. He is worth everything I have to give. He would tell me: "I feel fine when you're around." It's like he was writing the lyrics to this song!

Andy is doing so well now, and I am incredibly proud of him. If you didn't know Andy from before, you would never have suspected that he was fighting such demons during his college years. I think it's funny that Andy is so much like James in how he carries himself (quiet) and especially how he dresses! He wears 90 percent of the same clothing James wears. And of course, I love that!

There isn't a song that James sings that I don't like. His voice has been a part of my life for so long. "Copperline" has to be my favorite song. The words that James sings are so original and pure. But truly, every song has at least one line that speaks to my heart. His band is amazing too, all fabulous musicians in their own right. When Larry

Goldings toured with James, just the two of them, I saw the show twice, and could have enjoyed it a hundred times more.

Everyone who knows me knows how much I love James. Any news of him is texted or sent via social media almost immediately. Friends always ask me when he's coming to town, or if they know he's playing nearby soon, they'll say, "Better get your tickets!" (Like I haven't already had them for months!)

I have seen James soften through the years; his love for his family and friends is admirable. He is so humble, so kind, and so doggone funny! I was actually able to have a short conversation with him at a concert while he signed my 1979 copy of *Rolling Stone* with his picture on the cover. I was so happy to tell him: "Thank you. Thank you for sharing your voice with us."

I will always be grateful that he did not stop trying through all the rejections, the addictions, and the personal problems. He stayed true to his dream. And that allows us to dream.

Thank you. Thank you, James, for sharing your voice and your life with all of us.

CHAPTER 7

Don't Let Me Be Lonely Tonight

Sandy Matthews - Chicago, IL

In 1975, I heard my first James Taylor song. I was in my second year at North Central College in Naperville, Illinois, a school where African Americans students made up less than 3 percent of the student population. I came to the predominantly white campus prepared to learn and have new life experiences. I made new friends, and two young ladies, Janine Schaeffer and Sharon Bozwell, both white, became my best friends. We came from very different worlds but shared something that united us, and that was music.

Sharon played guitar, and we spent many evenings discussing our tastes in music. My favorites were soul, rhythm and blues, and jazz: Earth, Wind & Fire, Stevie Wonder, Aretha Franklin, Miles Davis, Ray Charles, and Smokie Robinson. My friends exposed me to rock, pop, and country, some of which I liked. But then there was James Taylor: a combination of folk, pop, soul, and a little bit of rock. On one of those evenings in my dorm back in 1975, the first James Taylor song I heard was "Don't Let Me Be Lonely Tonight."

That song spoke to me. I was sad, and at times lonely for my friends and family and all that was familiar to me. Even though I was experiencing new things and making new friends, I didn't feel fully accepted by many professors, students, and a particular (white) guy that I met on campus, both of us experiencing being attracted to a person outside of our race.

Then I discovered "Carolina In My Mind," "Fire And Rain," and so many more. James Taylor was then, and is still today, an amazing and unique artist.

I had the honor of meeting Mr. Taylor at the 2012 Democratic Convention. We were both in the Obama Friends and Family suite on the night of the Democratic Party presidential nominee acceptance speech. That was a night and an experience I will never forget.

CHAPTER 8

Enough To Be On Your Way

Cynthia Andrade – Vandalia, OH

When life gets overwhelming, I get in my car and cruise around listening to James Taylor tunes.

The first time I remember hearing JT was listening to "Sweet Baby James" in my friend's cool little attic bedroom under the eaves. As two high school girls, we would listen to that album for hours! Such a fond memory. I've been a fan ever since.

And then, a couple of years ago, I heard the song "Enough To Be On Your Way" from the *Hourglass* album (I'm still working on my JT album collection). The first time I heard the lyrics about carrying home in your heart, I was remembering some people close to me who have passed away. I was trying to deal with feelings and frustrations about some difficult family situations.

I connect even more now with that song during COVID-19, when home is an even more precious, safe place to be. I even have an idea in my mind for a needlework design I'd like to make, inspired by this song!

Thank you, James, for reminding me what "home" can be.

CHAPTER 9

Fire And Rain

Paul Adler – Chilmark, MA

The first time I heard a James Taylor album was in the summer of 1970, when my brother introduced me to "Fire And Rain." I was immediately mesmerized by the voice, lyrics, and musical composition. In the summer of 1971, I was 20 years old and attending WPI college in Worcester, Massachusetts. I remember riding my motorcycle to Martha's Vineyard to see if I could meet James. I was a part-time drummer, working my way through college with weekend gigs, and my dream was to jam with James someday. I asked some locals on Martha's Vineyard where James lived, and when I found his house, some carpenters were building a wood fence around the perimeter of his property. They were super friendly and said he was home, but I was too nervous to go knock on his door.

About a year later, James and Carole King played a concert at my college, Worcester Polytechnic, and of course I got a ticket. During the first part of the concert, I noticed drums on the stage, but no drummer. I walked up to the stage, paced back and forth, but could not get up the nerve to walk on stage and play with them during the show. I remember thinking, "What if I get kicked off before I even sit down at the drums?" The chance of getting humiliated in front of 5,000 concert goers was just too much.

After the show, I found the courage to go up to the road manager and told him I would like to meet James. He asked why, and I made up a story. I said I was one of the guys who painted his fence on Martha's Vineyard. A few minutes later, the road manager came back smiling and said James would like to meet me. I was obviously nervous, as I did not paint his fence. I was brought backstage, and found James waiting for me with his entire entourage listening. He smiled and said, "So you're the guy who painted my fence?" I quickly said, "No, not really." He smiled wider and said, "This is actually so funny because my fence was never painted!" I must have turned bright red and remember being so embarrassed.

I moved to Martha's Vineyard in 1978, became a carpenter, and played in several local bands and ultimately, some well-known bands. One experience I will never forget was the time I was able to jam with James at his brother Hugh's party at Dogfish Bar in the early 1980s. James, in disguise with a big top hat, asked to sit in with my band, but because of the disguise, I did not recognize him.

I let him play anyway, and he did not want to stop playing when the set was over. At some point in our set, I was behind James on drums and I remember saying, "You're really good, you should pursue a career in music." He slightly turned around and said, "You really think so?" I didn't find out it was James until after the gig. I am glad I did not know, or I would have probably played terribly from nerves.

Years later I became a concert promoter. I hosted Sally and Ben Taylor, Livingston Taylor, Carly Simon, Danny Kortchmar, and Arnold

McCuller in multiple solo concerts I produced on the Vineyard over twenty years, but never hosted James. I even had James's mother, Trudy, over my house for dinner a few times. I ended up getting more into the real estate business on the Vineyard so I can't complain about how my life has turned out, but to this day, almost fifty years later, I still wonder what would have happened had I knocked on James' door at his Lambert's Cove home in 1971 and introduced myself as a drummer.

⤳

Jordan Cook & Alicia Barry – Portsmouth, RI

When my mom told me she was taking me to my first concert, I planned my outfit for WEEKS. After what was probably an unreasonable amount of time at the mirror, I decided on a purple crocheted hat with double braids and my coolest overalls (yes, I realize now that that's an oxymoron) with tan work boots. To be fair, it was 1994 and this was a total look. I grew up with James Taylor playing in the house, so I knew who he was before we headed to Great Woods (now the Xfinity Center). But, like the lovely 12-year-old girl I was, I complained the entire drive up that we weren't seeing the New Kids on the Block.

I don't remember much from that concert, but I do remember that when I heard the music, I didn't care anymore that I wouldn't be getting up close and personal with Donnie Wahlberg. James' music just does something to you, pulls you in in such a way that you lose yourself and find yourself again—all at the same time. I can't recall the set list or if there were any guest musicians, but I do have a vivid memory of my mom taking my hand when she saw me smiling to say, "See, I told you you'd love it!"

I'm 37 years old and I still hate when my mom proves me wrong, but this was one of those moments frozen in time; and I will always treasure that show and that moment I shared with James Taylor and my mom.

Alicia Barry (Jordan's Mom)

When I read Jordan's recap of the time I took her to see James Taylor at Great Woods, I had a good laugh. She was miserable the entire drive and sulked the whole way there. I remember asking her to keep an open mind and shared with her my story of being a shy and sensitive 16-year-old girl who listened to his album, *Sweet Baby James*, over and over because it made me feel powerful in a way that I had not been able to express. I told her when I first heard "Fire And Rain" I cried for days because I felt as though I was "Suzanne" in the song. Jordan knew that I'd had a troubled childhood, with violence and uncertainty, and that I had battled depression. She became very quiet, and I could tell she was actually beginning to digest why I wanted to be in his presence.

As James walked on stage, I felt like that young lost girl again who was about to be comforted by his words and music. I reached over to Jordan's hand, and she let me clasp my hand in hers easily, which wasn't always the case in those days. I smiled at her through my 16-year-old eyes, although I was then 40, and we met in a place where there was no age but simply two girls swaying to music that moved us. As James began to sing "Fire And Rain," Jordan squeezed my hand and whispered to me, "I love you Mom," and I knew she understood.

Shawn Cullen – Wales, UK

I t was 1991. I was 16 years old. And it was the start of my "lovely ride."

I had just purchased Marc Cohn's eponymous debut album on a cassette tape. There were background vocals playing on one of the tracks—"Perfect Love"—and the tone of the voice was breathtaking. I searched through the liner notes and found it was an artist named James Taylor. I had never heard of him. Come on, I was 16, living in the UK, with parents who were into the likes of Billy Fury and Tom Jones!

I went out during my lunch hour and searched for something by this new artist I had discovered. In the UK there was a cassette release by James Taylor called *Classic Songs*.

"That will do," I thought.

When I got back home, I put the cassette in my Sony Walkman and placed the fluorescent sponge earphones over my eagerly awaiting ears.

The first song, just after the hiss, started.

A sliding acoustic guitar, with strings being picked, evoked a haunting tune.

The opening lyrics passed through my ears, hit my brain and entered my heart.

Just yesterday morning...

In that moment I knew I had found something phenomenal. Something honest. Something unique.

I rewound the cassette and listened to the song again.

And again.

And again.

In total, I listened to "Fire And Rain" five times. Dumbstruck by the devastating lyrics. Moved by the simple melody. Engulfed by the sheer emotion elicited from a short, simple tune.

That was the start. That was my induction to all things James Taylor.

From there on in, my JT journey just blossomed (so to speak).

The first time I saw him live was at the Barbican in London in January of 1998. James Taylor Online was becoming a "thing." I had enjoyed many chats in the JT chatroom, and a few of us had agreed to meet up in the Rat and Carrot pub in London before the show. It was fantastic finding individuals sharing one common value—the love of JT. The show was exquisite. Being a poor student at the time, the seats I could afford were way back. I was disappointed not to have a chance to shake JT's hand but felt blessed to have seen him live.

As my then girlfriend (now wife) and I left the auditorium, one of the Rat and Carrot posse came over to me and said, "Do you want to meet James Taylor?"

Of course, I replied *Yes!*

"Follow me," Stuart said, and Jules and I did just that.

We formed an orderly queue. And one by one we were ushered into a room where we were permitted a few minutes with James. I was tongue tied. All I could think of saying was "We've traveled all the way from Cardiff in Wales." JT asked, "How far is that?" "About two and a half hours on the train," I said. JT responded by saying "Shit!"

Yes, James Taylor swore at me. He then proceeded to tell me that he had been to Cardiff in the late 1960s and remembered it as a seaport.

I thanked him for allowing us to meet him and for the music. We shook hands, and Jules and I wandered off into the London night. All I kept saying during that night and the next day was, "I can't believe I just met James Taylor."

From 1998 to 2003. March 25, 2003 to be precise. My 29th birthday. Front row seats at the Mermaid Theatre in London in a special intimate concert recorded for BBC Radio 2. I managed to secure two tickets through a friend of a friend who worked for the BBC. There must have been two hundred people in the room at most. Walking down to our seat was wild. There were reserved seats for Terry Wogan, Whispering Bob Harris, and Jonathan Ross, to name but a few. The concert was so different because it was almost like JT playing in your living room.

A nice touch before the concert: My wife and I were sitting in a pub opposite the theatre before the show. And as we sipped our drinks, who should walk in, one by one? Every member of JT's band. Every single one. They sat down and proceeded to chill in what appeared to be a pre-show ritual.

Since then, we've seen him play in Birmingham, Alabama, for his *One Man Band* show; on the grounds of Edinburgh Castle (July 2004); in the Olympia Music Hall in Paris (May 2012); in the Auditorium Conciliazione in Rome (February 1998); several times in Cardiff and venues throughout the UK; and some wonderful front row center seats in one of the most wonderful venues in the world: The Royal Albert Hall in London (October 2014).

Every show. Every performance. Every ounce of JT's being leaves my jaw firmly on the floor when he plays live. He clearly loves doing it. Loves his audience. And loves to give back.

I am waiting with bated breath for his next UK or European tour. You never know how long an artist will keep going through the punishing schedule of a tour. But as long as JT keeps showing up, so will I.

❦

Barb Heizman - Greenwood, MO

One afternoon in the early 1970s, I heard some pretty music coming out of my sister Beth's bedroom, so I went to her doorway to listen. "Who is that?" I asked.

She held up an album sleeve showing a man with long hair and bangs down to his eyes lying in the grass. "James Taylor," she said. I thought he was cute, but the voice—it was so endearing.

Not long after that I found myself at a local music store buying an Alvarez guitar with nylon strings, along with the James Taylor *Sweet Baby James* songbook. Using the chords in the back of the book, I taught myself to play. Soon, I played well enough that the choir director at my high school asked me to sit in the orchestra for our production of *The Sound of Music*.

In 1983, when I saw that James was scheduled to play in August at the Starlight Theater in Kansas City, I bought season tickets to be sure that I wouldn't miss him. But it wasn't meant to be. In June, my husband's ex-wife died in a horrible car wreck, and their two little boys were badly hurt, so I spent the rest of my summer caring for the boys' broken arms, legs, and head injuries. Throughout the summer, one by one, I gave my tickets away. When it came close to the date for James' show, I knew I couldn't go, so I gave the tickets to my sister Beth. I was glad I could pass them on to the person who had introduced me to James Taylor so many years ago. During this time, I learned how to make quilts; it was a way to relieve stress and feed my artistic soul at the same time.

In 1992, my father died by suicide. "Fire And Rain" provided a deep sense of comfort to me during that time, and I listened to it again and again, along with so many other JT songs. I was inspired to write a song called "Distant Moon" about how even when someone isn't with you any longer in the flesh, they still are with you in spirit. I had the song professionally produced, copyrighted it, and decided to try to get a demo to James. I called the university where I knew that James' father was teaching but was told that he had recently retired. To my surprise, they gave me his address in Boston and his phone number.

I called the number and was greeted by "Dr. Taylor." I told him who I was and what I was hoping to do. When I asked how he was doing, he told me "not well" and went on to tell me that James' step-mom had just died of cancer. But rather than ending the conversation, he asked if I wanted James' address. He laid down the phone and came back to give it to me. I was so excited to have James' address, and I mailed the demo right away. Though I never got a response, I was left with such fond memories of how sweet Dr. Taylor was to me that day on the phone.

A few years later, in 1998, Beth died of cancer. Once again, the song "Fire And Rain" came to my rescue as a source of deep comfort. In Beth's obituary, James was listed as one of her greatest loves. I wrote James a letter telling him this, but this time I didn't mail it, I wanted to give it to him in person. James was set to play in Little Rock, Arkansas, so I got tickets and drove seven hours from Kansas City to Little Rock. During intermission, I made my way to the stage to hand him the letter. But for some reason, he shook his head and wouldn't take it, so I put it down on the stage, hoping he would pick it up after the show. Unfortunately, he never did, so I took the letter back home with me.

I was still determined to tell James my story. I had an idea that if I made him a quilt, it would show my love and appreciation for him. I was busy raising the last of my five kids, and I also worked full time, so I didn't have much time for quilting.

But in 2005, my mother died, and I decided to take some time off. My boys and I moved to an old farmhouse and I finally had the time to begin the quilt. I spent long hours into the night sewing, stopping only for a few hours of sleep. I'd never embroidered before, but I illustrated twelve of his songs by "painting with thread." When it was done, I mailed it to someone who promised to give it to James. It wasn't long

before I received a photo of James all wrapped up in it. That warmed my heart.

The following year, James' assistant contacted me and offered me tickets to a show in St. Louis, along with backstage passes for me and my two sons. Of course, I said yes! When I met James and told him I was the woman who made the quilt, he threw his arms around me and gave me a tight hug. He said he'd been thinking about me, and we spent a long time chatting, together with my sons.

Over the next fifteen years, I've had many opportunities to talk with James at intermission, or after a show. One of the most memorable was in Des Moines, Iowa. After the show, I waited with twenty or so people out by the buses to see if we could chat with him. When he walked out, he spoke with fans, shook hands, and signed autographs. When he saw me, he came straight over and gave me a kiss on my forehead. I drove home after the show, with my sunroof opened, and looking up at the stars, I cried "Beth, that kiss was for YOU!"

When I was diagnosed with breast cancer in 2016 and told James that I had surgery but refused chemo, he spent a good fifteen minutes with me trying to convince me to listen to the doctors. I told him if God wanted me here, I'd be here. "Don't worry about me," I told James.

The cancer came back every spring for three years, but last year, it was gone. Today, it is still gone. I believe the anticipation and excitement of looking forward to James' concerts helps me stay upbeat and very much alive.

My life has been SO much richer for knowing James Taylor.

Thank you, James.

༄

Sarah Ann Mayfield - Joplin, MO

I was in my twenties when I first became a James Taylor fan. My mother-in-law, Judy, had purchased a CD of James' *Greatest Hits*. I remember going on a long car trip with her and drifting to sleep to those mellow tunes. I had no idea that those songs would become the soundtrack, not only to my life, but also to my children's' lives.

On June 1, 2005, my mother-in-law passed away. This was unexpected, and it rocked our world. I was emotionally devastated, as I had known Judy since I was ten years old. She considered me her daughter, and I thought of her as a second mom. The days following her death were full of heartache and tears. I recall sitting at a computer and searching on YouTube for the song "Fire And Rain." I sat there, tears flowing down my face, listening and feeling all the regrets, "should haves," and "if onlys." The lyrics resonated in my soul.

For weeks, I sat and played "Fire And Rain" on repeat as memories of our time together played in my mind like a video accompanying the lyrics. As time passed, I continued to listen almost daily, but I cried less. Then, I started to expand my interest in James Taylor, letting YouTube suggest other songs. I fell in love with them, just as I had with "Fire And Rain," "Sweet Baby James," "Carolina In My Mind," and "You've Got A Friend" would come to be important songs in my life for different reasons.

In 2007, I had my fourth and final child, Megan. I was alone a lot of the time, as my husband worked nights. I was listening to music to keep me company, day in and day out. I would feed Megan and play "Sweet Baby James." It became her lullaby and to this day, at 12 years old, she will tell you: "That's my lullaby!"

As the years moved on, our lives did too. My kids were all growing up with a love for music. I was still actively listening to James, especially at night as the household would quiet down to prepare for sleep. Megan was still falling asleep to "Sweet Baby James," and I would drift off to "You Can Close Your Eyes."

In 2013, we moved our family to Alaska. We were suddenly 4,000 miles from home, and I was homesick! I lay in bed at night, listening to Carole King's, "So Far Away" and James' beautiful song, "Carolina In My Mind," and I would cry. I felt like it had been penned just for me. I was making friends, and I had my family, but I still felt so isolated and alone. I missed home; I missed all I had ever really known. These songs were the balm over my broken heart.

We left Alaska in 2015, and I missed those friends, the same as I missed my friends from Missouri. The lyrics still strike a melancholy chord for me, even today.

In 2016, James Taylor brought his *All-Star Band* tour to Springfield, Missouri. I lived an hour away, and my husband at the time could not take off work for the show. We had only one car, so I didn't even try to figure out how to attend. But then, I got a message from my husband's stepmother telling me they had tickets given to them, and I could even bring all the kids. My father-in-law graciously offered to drive the hour to pick us up and take us to the concert.

I was elated! This was a dream come true, not only for me, but for my daughter, Madalynn, who is an aspiring musician, and for Megan. My sons also agreed to go, though they didn't seem to grasp the significance to me.

I was thrilled to be going to this show and sharing it with the most important people in my life, my children. That night was a night I will never forget. I sang along to every song. I cried as I watched Megan tearfully sing "Sweet Baby James." She was so moved to be hearing it in person that she cried, too. At 8 years old, she was one of the youngest in the venue. I have tears as I remember this, even today.

I held Madalynn's hand as we cried and sang along to "Fire And Rain." I saw my sons singing along, and my heart was full. What started with their grandmother's love of James Taylor had now found three generations at a show together. It could only have been better if Judy could have joined us. It was a night I will never forget.

Music is a common denominator for many. Whatever the genre, whatever the decade, it is a force that binds humankind together. There is a camaraderie in standing among thousands of fellow fans in awe of the performer, and just living in the moment.

So, Mr. Taylor, if you ever read this, please know that you have made a difference. You have impacted many. From the old to the young, your words mean something. They resonate deep in the spirit and they make a difference in the lives of those taking the time to listen. I always hope I'll see you, one more time again.

You are the music of my life. Thank you for your gift.

Patricia Harris Miller – Franklin, IN

The first song I ever heard James Taylor sing was "Fire And Rain" and I was hooked immediately. In the early 1970s, I saw him for the first time in concert with Carly Simon at Butler University in Indianapolis, Indiana. I haven't missed a James Taylor concert in forty-six years (and have brought him roses to every show), even when I was scheduled to start chemotherapy in 2001. I told my doctor, "I have third row, center stage tickets, and I won't risk being

sick and missing James." Luckily, my doctor was a James Taylor fan too. He smiled and said, "Well, let's get you rescheduled for after the show."

James' music has been in my life for as long as I can remember. At my prom, we danced to "Don't Let Me Be Lonely Tonight." Forty-two years

ago, at my wedding, we played his music at the reception and danced all night. When I started having babies, we played James' music in the surgical suite during my C-section. And then, years later as my daughter had her C-section, we voted on which CD should be playing for her. She chose the *Troubadour Reunion* album and delivered a healthy, happy baby. In July, for my birthday every year, I buy tickets for my mother, sisters, and daughters so we can all enjoy the James Taylor experience together. I told them, "If I die tomorrow, at least you'll know what good music sounds like."

Even my 84-year-old mother loves James. She recently knitted him a beautiful deep green and blue scarf (using my father as a model to make it the right length). Inside, she sewed her "made special from Irene" label. She keeps asking me if I think he wears it.

James, thank you for all the tunes and concerts and the love and kindness you show to your fans. I love it when you see me, and you call me out by my first name. Thank you for signing albums and pictures and Rolling Stone magazines and for always taking pictures with us. Like you, I have battled depression for many years. I love all your music, but I'm particularly drawn to your darker, more melancholy tunes; those songs have saved my life. You are humble and kind, and I will always remember each and every encounter with a smile. Thank you.

❧

Ken Montigny - Fairhaven, MA

I was raised on good music and started playing guitar at four years old. (I still own that guitar today!) My father played guitar and had a fondness for the Laurel Canyon sound and the folk rock coming out of the 1960s. I grew up listening to Crosby, Stills & Nash, The Mamas and the Papas, and Joni Mitchell, but the one that hit a chord for me, so to speak, was James Taylor.

The first time I heard a James Taylor song was when my father played "Fire And Rain" for me on his guitar. He interpreted the lyrics and played the music in his own style of chord shapes, a style of open tuning similar to that of Richie Havens. He loved that song and identified with the message of life's challenges and perseverance, and with great patience he taught me how to play "Fire And Rain" the same way he had.

In my early teens, I began my own journey of learning the guitar, and abandoned the open tuning my father had taught me. James Taylor's music was essential in developing my skills. I spent countless hours trying to recreate the nuance that is unique to James' playing in songs like "Carolina In My Mind" and "Something In The Way She Moves."

His playing and chord structure evolved into even more complex chord blending in the 1990s in songs such as "Like Everyone She Knows" and "Enough To Be On Your Way." This evolution was a wonderful challenge for me, and I took it on, year after year.

In addition to playing his music on guitar, I found that over the years my voice has naturally matured to be very close in timber to the classic baritone quality of James' voice. I spent years as a solo performer that always included several of James' songs in my set list. It became what I was known for. I was the guy that played and sounded like James Taylor. At the urging of my good friend and musical partner for the past forty years, in 2016 we assembled a seven-piece James Taylor Tribute band called October Road. (And did you notice my Ted Williams hat? The same one that James often wears!)

I have been fortunate to be able to surround myself with some of the best players in Southern New England who share my love for James Taylor's songbook. Today, October Road plays at numerous summer concert series and theaters throughout Massachusetts and Rhode Island. "Fire And Rain" is *always* on the set list. Performing that song comes from a very special place in my heart.

My father passed away just over twenty years ago, but I know he would have been thrilled to see me play the song he taught me so many years ago.

∽

Darren Moreash – Nova Scotia, Canada

When I was young, I listened to hard rock almost exclusively. It was not until my late twenties when a few musicians veered me away for a bit: the Beatles, Joni Mitchell, Gordon Lightfoot, and of course, James Taylor.

James Taylor is the reason I started playing acoustic guitar. His finger picking was so smooth; it was unlike anything I had ever heard. The song "Fire And Rain" made me buy a guitar tab book.

If nothing else, I had to learn the beginning of that song.

Around that same time, I started carving wooden marionettes, just for fun. My girlfriend wanted one, so I went to the library and checked out a couple of books about marionette making. I taught myself how to carve, pretty much trial and error. The one I made for my girlfriend was of ME. She liked it so much she kept it ... even after she got rid of me; it must have been less annoying.

In 2016, I found out James Taylor was coming to Halifax for a show, and I knew I had to go. I carved a wooden marionette of James and decided to try and contact him. It wasn't easy, but with the internet and social media at least I had somewhere to start. I messaged his website, waited, and hoped for the best while expecting ... well ... nothing. But the stars aligned, and someone messaged me back! They said James would love to meet me and see the marionette and extended an invitation, along with tickets to the show.

The concert was, as I expected, amazing. It was separated into two sets. The coolest thing was that during intermission when the band went backstage, James did not. He spent the entire break sitting on the edge of the stage signing stuff for anyone who could reach him. I'd never seen anything like that before, especially from an icon.

After the show, I went backstage with a few other lucky people to meet him. I showed him the marionette, and he loved it. He couldn't stop playing with it! We snapped a few photos, and he signed a lyric sheet of "Fire And Rain" I had printed out. James' management told me to send a few photos of the meet up and they'd post it on their Twitter page, which they did!

It was an amazing, memorable evening I will never forget.

Laurie Savioli – North Attelboro, MA

My love for James Taylor started in the first grade. I remember hanging out with my grandfather and listening to music with him after school. He played all kinds of music, but for some reason, James really stood out to me.

47

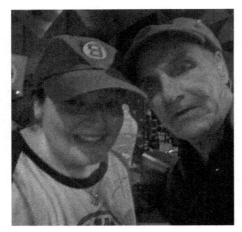

Soon, I became known as the girl who loved James Taylor. I grew up using AOL Instant Messenger, so while my classmates had new pop songs in their profiles, I was quoting "Copperline" and other James Taylor songs. On my eighteenth birthday, my friend decorated my locker in the senior hallway with pictures of James, along with a Happy Birthday sign. I left school early that day to see Livingston Taylor play at a Borders Bookstore. (I love Liv, too!)

To this day, people call or text me if they hear that James is going to be somewhere, or if they see him on TV. My dad even used to call me when he was driving and heard a JT song. He wouldn't say anything—he just put the phone up to the speaker.

JT's music speaks to my soul. I have a song for every emotion and situation. I still remember the morning my grandfather died; I heard "Fire And Rain" playing on Magic 106.7. I felt heartbroken, but also felt like the song was a sign for me, and it was comforting. I often base my day on hearing a James Taylor song or not. I love all his top hits, but I am happiest when I hear the lesser known ones.

For years and years my goal was to meet James. I collected three James Taylor autographs before I got one for myself. On Wednesday, July 4th, 2018, I finally got my own at Tanglewood. During intermission, James was signing autographs and taking selfies. I had already cried during the entire show because I was third row center and I thought nothing could ever top that experience. Andrea Zonn, who sings backup and plays the fiddle, totally caught me crying. During intermission, I was pushed and pulled trying to make my way to JT sitting on stage, and I thought there was no way I'd make it to him. When I finally did, I stood there sobbing, as he signed my shirt and ticket. Then he took my phone out of my hands and took a selfie. I ugly cried and told him I loved him.

The one thing I had hoped and prayed for over the course of twenty-plus years had happened. I honestly thought it never would, and to this day, I cannot believe it. Sometimes I will randomly think about it and cry. I remember posting pictures on Facebook and writing that I finally met James Taylor. People I haven't spoken to since elementary school "liked" and "loved" the post.

Honestly, there's no way to put into words what James means to me, what he's gotten me through, or how he's changed my life. It's amazing how his music speaks to me, how it can help me come down from an anxiety attack or hype me up when I need it. He is someone who will never get to know the effect he's had on my life. He may not know it, but I do. I am forever thankful for him and I will ALWAYS hold a special place for him in my heart.

❧

Anna Tripp – St. Simons Island, GA

I was 10 years old the first time I heard the song "Fire And Rain" on my AM/FM radio. I remember sitting in my bedroom in Augusta, Georgia, and my world stopped. I fell instantly in love with that voice. That was the beginning of my love for James Taylor.

James Taylor's music speaks to me. Whether I'm happy or sad, I welcome a JT song. When I hear one of his songs, it takes me back to a specific place and time, just like "Fire And Rain" takes me back to my childhood bedroom.

James' music is an integral part of my life and brings me so much joy. A few years ago, my sweet husband bought the best anniversary gift: tickets to see James when he was touring with Carole King (my other all-time favorite). That was one of the most joyful experiences I've ever had in my 57 years.

God bless James for pulling himself out of the darkness years ago. If he hadn't, he might not be here today to share the God-given talent that has brought me and thousands of others decades of joy. I'm forever grateful for his music.

CHAPTER 10

Get A Job

Shana Lewis - Philadelphia, PA

I am 27 years old, and it's hard to tell exactly how my love of James Taylor started. This is a little embarrassing to recall, but my mother used to write down every single "funny" thing I said when I was younger. When I was four years old, one choice statement was: "I forgot James Taylor's name."

While I don't remember *that* in particular, I do remember listening to James Taylor CDs when driving to New York with my parents to do modeling gigs. On many of those trips we listened to James Taylor's *New Moon Shine* CD, and I've had a nostalgic attachment to that album ever since. I also have fond childhood memories of watching a taped recording of *Squibnocket*.

After eighteen years of being a fan of his music, my time to see him in concert finally came on June 10, 2010, and then again just a few days later, on June 22. It was the *Troubadour Reunion* tour with Carole King, and I loved every second of both shows. My third concert, on August 1, 2015 at the Borgata in Atlantic City, was memorable for the fact that I got to see James spend the intermission signing autographs.

My fourth JT concert also included random encounters with fans. It was the show with Bonnie Raitt on July 7, 2017. It was a pretty amazing experience, because Bonnie was my dad's favorite singer and JT is mine, and it was my first time seeing them share a stage.

Those concert memories are wonderful, for sure. But the greatest thing that ever happened to me because of becoming a James Taylor fan had to be buying his *Covers* album. When I saw that the track listing on the bonus disc included the 1958 hit, "Get A Job" by The Silhouettes, a doo wop group that my late father, Richard Lewis, sang with, I couldn't believe it. My dad wrote the song and was the tenor voice in the band. He passed away in 2005, when I was 13.

Someday I hope to meet James Taylor and thank him for covering that song and bringing back fond memories of my father to me.

CHAPTER 11

Handy Man

Max Tosi – Milan, Italy

The first time I heard James Taylor was in 1980, when I was a carefree 17-year-old "man." The song was "Handy Man."

My first JT concert was in Milan at the Arena in July of 2007, and then again in Cagliari (Sardinia) at the Lyrical Theatre on JT's birthday, March 12, 2012. The last and most memorable concert I attended was at Milan's Arcimboldi Theatre in April of 2015.

I'm a songwriter also, and I play James Taylor songs all the time as a tribute to his artistry. Some of my favorite lyrics are from the songs "Shower The People," "Enough To Be On Your Way," and "Gaia." In 2008 I tried to send my first album to him through an Irish friend of mine, but I don't think it ever arrived.

I took my first picture with James in Milan in 2015; I had waited outside the theater for about an hour and a half,

finally got my picture with him but was too shy to even talk! He was exactly like I expected, a shy person, simple, polite, and full of patience with his fans.

I believe that James' music has changed my life, and not just musically. I can't put it properly in words, but I will say that his music has made me grow as both a musician and songwriter.

CHAPTER 12

How Sweet It Is [To Be Loved By You]

Rebecca Lyn Gold - Newport, RI

In June of 1977, my best friend, Sean, told me that he would figure out a way we could get into the outdoor concert at Fort Adams in Newport, Rhode Island, where James Taylor was rumored to be a surprise guest. That was just the kind of guy Sean was. He knew I had been through hell the past few years, dealing with my parents' divorce, changing schools, and losing a big part of my family and friends in the midst of it all. The only thing that kept me grounded was the music of James Taylor. Sean knew I loved James Taylor, and that I had never seen him in concert, so this would be a dream come true.

"How are we gonna get in?" I asked. "It's been sold out forever."

"I'll figure out a way," he said. "Trust me."

THAT'S WHY WE'RE HERE

I didn't bring it up again, but I kept counting down the days to the concert, even though we didn't yet have tickets, and I wasn't exactly hopeful that we would get any.

On the morning of the concert date, Sean called and told me he'd be at my house at 10:00 a.m., so be ready.

"Oh, and wear a black skirt and a white blouse," he said. "We're going to see JT!"

"What? Are you kidding me?"

"Does it sound like I'm kidding? Go, get ready! I'll be there in ten."

When Sean showed up wearing black pants and a white shirt, holding a tray of uncooked chicken legs and a bucket of potato salad, my mom broke out in laughter.

"What the heck are you up to?" she exclaimed.

"Meet James Taylor's new catering company!" he announced.

"What?" I said. "Are you serious?"

"C'mon," he said. "Get dressed. We gotta go!"

"Wouldn't it be better if it were cooked?" Mom asked.

"Well, yeah, that would help. Are you offering?"

"Sure, I can cook it," my mother said. She took out some barbeque sauce from the fridge and salt-and-peppered the legs and put them in the oven. "It's going to take forty-five minutes," she said. "And give me that bucket of potato salad so I can put it in a nice bowl and spice it up a bit."

If there was one thing my mother knew how to do well, it was to dress up any food to make it look better than it even tasted. She reached into the highest kitchen cabinet where she kept her fancy serving trays. "Here's a nice one you can use for the chicken," she said, brushing off a brightly colored ceramic tray. "Get out the romaine and fresh parsley from the fridge," she instructed Sean, who somehow knew exactly what she was up to. "And slice up some radishes, too."

"Yes, ma'am," Sean said, giggling. "Radicchio coming right up!" Then he waved to me. "Go, get dressed. We got this."

I left the two of them dancing around the kitchen and went to my room to find a black and white outfit. This could work, I thought. This could actually work!

About a half hour later Sean and I were ready to leave with our beautifully decorated tray full of barbequed chicken, along with a large bowl of garnished potato salad.

"What about plates and napkins?" I asked.

"Got it covered," he said. "They're in the car."

"Don't you dare use paper napkins!" my mother exclaimed. "Here, take these." She handed me a stack of bright red flowered cloth napkins with a bag of gold beaded napkin rings. "These will look nice."

"Perfect," Sean said. "Carly loves poppies."

"How do you know?" I asked.

"Let's just go," he said, pushing me out the door. "Leave the details to me." He smiled. "Thanks, Barbara!" he called as we walked out.

"Good luck!" she called back.

I felt so happy, truly happy, happier than I had felt in a very long time. I had a real friend, my mother helped us do something pretty cool, and we were on our way to see James Taylor in concert! Things hadn't looked this good in a very, very long time.

When we got to Fort Adams, Sean immediately saw someone he knew working at one of the food stands at the venue, so when we got to the front gate without tickets but holding a tray of cooked chicken, Sean waved to the guy and we walked right in like we owned the place.

I walked behind him with my head held high, and we walked right to the backstage entrance. "Excuse me, excuse me, we are the caterers, and we have James Taylor's barbeque. Please let us through!"

"Who are you?" The security guy pulled out a piece of paper with a bunch of names on it.

"Oh hey, Dan!" Sean answered. "Don't worry, I've got yours right here. You're a breast man, aren't ya?" Sean laughed, grabbed one of the paper plates, put a thick juicy barbequed chicken breast on it and scooped out some potato salad. "Keep it quiet now, right? We don't have enough for all your guys."

Dan chuckled, folded the piece of paper in his hand and took the plate of food from Sean. "You got it," he said. "Go on ahead. The Taylors are right over there."

Later, I asked Sean how he knew the security guard. He said, "Is it so hard to read a name badge?"

As we made our way to the front of the backstage area, directly behind the curtains that hadn't yet opened, there were several stage crew hands bustling around getting ready for the show. Out of the corner of my eye I saw James Taylor tuning his guitar. I stopped dead in my tracks. "Sean," I nudged him. "Look, there he is."

"Oh, good," he said. "Follow me."

And so I followed him, right to where James was sitting on a chair tuning his guitar, and Carly Simon was sitting on a bench with their two young children, Sally and Ben, who were dancing around her, laughing and singing. She was stunning, with her long flowing hair cascading down her lace top. She was even more beautiful in person than I could have imagined. And her legs! It was hard to keep my eyes off them. She sat there calmly giggling at the children, who were running around in circles attempting to make themselves dizzy, then falling to their butts and laughing.

"Hey there, kiddos," Sean said. "How about some chicken?"

"Oh, that's great," said Carly. "Here kids, time to take a break." She got up from the bench and scooped up Ben from the floor. "Time to eat, little one."

I put the tray of chicken and potato salad on the table and prepared a plate for the kids. I had to keep telling myself: *These are James Taylor's children. I am cutting chicken for James Taylor's children.*

Meanwhile, Sean, as comfortable as ever, was chatting with Carly like she was a long lost aunt, talking about her garden in her home in Martha's Vineyard. "You know what would be perfect in your front yard?" he said. "Peonies."

"Oh, I love peonies!" Carly exclaimed. "But I never have luck growing them."

"It's not so hard," Sean said. "Here's what you gotta do …" And he sat right down next to Carly Simon, THE Carly Simon, and gave her a lesson on how to grow the perfect peony in New England. Before long they were chatting and laughing like they were long lost friends.

Meanwhile, I was in a trance watching James out of the corner of my eye get ready for his performance. Ben and Sally were now throwing chicken pieces at each other while their nanny was frantically trying to continue feeding them.

I couldn't keep my eyes off James. With his guitar on his back, he was walking back and forth, his head bowed, getting in the zone. He was wearing a blousy white shirt and wide legged pants. He was taller than I imagined, a lot taller. But he didn't look up once, just kept his head down walking back and forth. I was mesmerized.

Suddenly there seemed to be crew everywhere trying to move people away from the curtain area. It was obviously show time.

"Come here," Sean said. "Let's sit over there." He grabbed the near empty tray of chicken, led me over to the side of the stage, and sat down on a bench. "No one will notice us here."

Just then, the curtains opened, the crowd roared, and James walked out. "Hi," he said softly into the microphone, and the crowd roared again. Then he strapped his guitar around him, sat on the stool in the middle of the stage, and started to play and sing..

"This is the best day of my entire life," I told Sean.

He smiled and put his arm around me. "Yeah, it's a good one," he said.

"You have no idea how much this means to me, Sean" I said.

"Be quiet or we'll get kicked out," he whispered. "Enjoy the show."

Carly and the kids were off in the distance, and everyone else backstage seemed to have found a spot to sit and were watching and listening. And there we were, the two of us, with our empty tray of barbequed chicken and bowl of half-eaten potato salad on the floor in front of us, watching and listening to James Tayor, THE James Taylor, just ten feet in front of us.

Sean and I have remained lifelong friends. Since that first concert, I have seen James more times than I can count, but you never forget your first.

How very sweet it is.

&

Amy Montuori – Pompano Beach, FL

The first time I heard a James Taylor song I was 15 years old. It was 1971 and I remember sitting on the shag carpet at a friend's house when the song "Sweet Baby James" came on the radio. I instantly loved it and was trying to sing along, but my friend told me I couldn't sing JT because my voice was too high, while hers, *of course*, was in the right octave.

I soon became a huge fan, and now I have many memories of JT concerts and songs. In the 1990s, I went to a JT concert at the Garden State Arts Center in New Jersey. As James came on stage, there were threatening clouds, and as soon as he played the first note, lightening hit the generator. The concert was over before it started.

Luckily, I've had many other opportunities to see JT in concert by himself, with Carole King at NYC's Madison Square Garden, and most recently, with Jackson Browne at Wrigley Field in Chicago. Whenever I hear a James Taylor song, a video plays in my mind of a time in my life I relate the song to. Like when I went to Florida with three girlfriends two months before I got married in July 1981. While we were driving through North Carolina, the song "Carolina In My Mind" came on the local radio station. We were singing it all together cramped in her little Toyota and we were so happy being together! What a great memory.

When I was a preschool teacher (for forty years) and an enrichment teacher for half-day kindergarten classes, I taught a class called "World Traveler." When we learned about Mexico, I taught the kids James' song "Mexico." They loved it so much and sang the chorus over and over. One night I received a phone call from one mother who told me her twins wouldn't stop singing that song, and it was driving her crazy! Those twins are now 18 years old and it seems like they were 5 just yesterday.

Of all the James Taylor songs, my favorite would be "How Sweet It Is (To Be Loved By You)" because it makes me feel how special it is to have been loved by my wonderful husband for thirty-five years. Thank you, James, for all the memories that each of your songs has brought to my life.

༄

Brandy Starr Ringle – Walker, MN

In the early 1980s, when my junior high school choir really wanted to sing songs by Madonna, or Prince, or Michael Jackson, we were singing songs by the Beatles, The Fifth Dimension, and the song "You've Got A Friend" written by Carole King and made famous by James Taylor. I'm thankful to our director, Mr. Strandlie, for "making" us sing the songs that still occupy my brain to this day, nearly forty years later.

Soon after learning to sing "You've Got A Friend," I made it my mission in life to find out as much as I could about James Taylor. I've spent the years since junior high collecting James Taylor songs and stories, and learning tidbits about this man, his life, and his music. It doesn't seem much of a mystery to me as to why I carry James Taylor's music in my soul. I was born in March

THAT'S WHY WE'RE HERE

1971, when many of his songs were born, or at least becoming popular. I am grateful to have been raised during such an amazing era of music!

When I think about my childhood, I remember listening to "Fire And Rain," "Sweet Baby James," and "Carolina In My Mind" and more JT songs all the time, whether on the radio, the turntable, or blasting out of the cassette player in the Fiat convertible I drove in high school. I feel very blessed to have these songs as a part of my life in those everyday moments, and even when times were difficult or sad.

If you were to ask my children about their childhood memories, they would tell you about James Taylor songs wafting up from the lake as their mama sat on the dock making jewelry in the summer sunshine. When my son was considering a song for the mother-son dance at his wedding, it was an easy choice: "How Sweet It Is (To Be Loved By You)." My oldest daughter did her senior project using JT songs. My second daughter sings JT songs and plays them on the piano, too.

When my youngest child was in preschool, her teacher called me to say that during playtime they had the radio on, and she announced to her schoolmates that the song playing was "How Sweet It Is" by James Taylor. She was four years old; she made her mama proud!

In June of 2016, I brought my 9-year-old daughter to her first concert—James Taylor, of course! We had floor seats about twenty rows from the stage. When it was close to intermission, I remembered that sometimes James will stay on stage and sign autographs, take pictures, and talk to fans. I took my child by her hand and off we went to the stage. At one point there were so many people that I had to pick her up and carry her as we edged our way among all the fans. Then, suddenly, I was reaching my hand out to James!

I held my daughter on my left hip and patted James on his bent knee with my right hand. He was sitting on stage talking to a baby being held by her mother. The only words I could get out of my mouth were "James, James, James." Finally, he turned to my daughter and me. "Hello there!" he said. "There are so many babies here tonight!"

James signed my daughter's forearm, her new JT tank top, and the sleeve of my jean jacket. His signature still lives on that jean jacket, right above his son Ben's. Then, just as quickly as it started, it was over, and he was on to greet someone else. I said, "Wait! Can I get a picture?"

James turned back to me and leaned down as I clumsily grabbed my phone and took a selfie with him, while still holding my daughter. The picture is ridiculous! It makes me laugh when I look at it; he looks great and I look like a deer caught in headlights.

I have always said that if I were able to have a conversation with James, the only thing I would want to say is "Thank You! Thank you, James, for your songs. Thank you, James, for your music! Thank you, James, for touring. Thank you, James, for getting clean. Thank you, James, for surviving. Thank you, James Taylor, thank you!"

CHAPTER 13

Like Everyone She Knows

Mary Kelley – Barkhamsted, CT

My story begins in 1978, when a friend of mine introduced me to Billy Kelley. My first impression of Billy was that he was loud, funny, and cute as heck. Later, he shared his thoughts—he had the exact same first impression of me. We were both fans of James Taylor, and as our love grew, so did our love for James' music.

We were married in October of 1981. It was the happiest day of my life. I had fallen in love with the kindest, sweetest, strongest man that I had ever met. On top of that, my mom loved him like a son. They always had a wonderful bond.

James' music had become a part of our marriage, and oh, what a marriage it was. We listened to him often, and I hope that this doesn't make my children blush, but his music was definitely playing when Billy and I fooled around!

We were blessed with three wonderful children. Our first child, Lisa Marie, was born in September of 1983. Our second child, Jeffrey Frederick, was born in August of 1985. And in May of 1992, we were absolutely shocked and surprised when my obstetrician introduced us to our third child. I had an ultrasound the day before his birth, and my doctor told us that our baby was a girl. Billy and I named her Maureen Rose. I packed the sweet little pink outfit that Lisa had worn home from the hospital in my bag and took it when I went to have our little girl. Boy, were we surprised when Maureen Rose turned out to be an adorable baby boy ... without a name! We settled on Peter Justin.

James Taylor's music continued to be a warm place where Billy and I could go as we lived our love story, raising our children. Billy was a wonderful father. There was nothing that he wouldn't do for our children, and they knew it.

Our love story took a terrible hit in April of 1992 when Billy was diagnosed with lung cancer. We dealt with his diagnosis in completely opposite ways. Billy did not see this as a fatal disease. Rather, he saw his cancer that something that could be managed and treated. It would go away, period. Meanwhile, I had had the rug pulled out from underneath me, and I never felt secure again.

Billy underwent surgery in 1992 and had the lower two lobes of his right lung removed. The nodes in his sternum were positive for cancer cells, so the next step was back to radiation. It burned his esophagus so badly that Billy would chug Mylanta—cherry flavor to be exact—trying to get some relief from the discomfort. My mom, equally devastated by his disease process, always made sure that he had enough Mylanta. He loved her for it.

Billy spent the next four years of his life undergoing chemotherapy and radiation. When he went for chemo, we asked that James Taylor be played at the cancer center, and the nurses obliged. It allowed us to both go into our own safe place. He calmly dealt with every physical symptom. Meanwhile, I was screaming inside. I prayed so hard for God not to take him. I prayed that God let us keep our family together. I prayed that he wouldn't die in pain. My solace was listening to James Taylor's music.

Just short of four years after his diagnosis, my husband, best friend, and forever love died. I was with him in his ICU bed in our local hospital. Our families were gathered there. His sister, who lived in Texas, had flown in that morning. I thanked his mother for sharing his life with me. His nurses were friends of mine, and they couldn't have worked harder to keep Billy comfortable.

I remember singing to him quietly, and I am sure quite off key, James' song "Like Everyone She Knows." We both loved that song.

It was about holding our family and his desire to live tight in our hearts. It was about not giving up. Billy never gave up, ever. It was about taking care of our family, embracing it tightly, like he had. And I think that the end of this verse told him to be patient—that things would be OK. He was. He was OK in the end.

I do have to share that the verse about tending your own fire was particularly meaningful to me. Billy was the fire department chief in our town when he died. He had been a member for almost twenty years. He had wonderful support from his fellow firefighters, true friends till the very end.

And so, we laid Billy to rest in his hometown cemetery, buried behind his father who had passed away ten years earlier. On Billy's headstone I had the above verse engraved.

Our children have not seen their Dad in twenty-four years. I have not seen or heard Billy's voice in twenty-four years. It has not been an easy road.

I look forward to being together with him again one day.

Thank you, James Taylor; if you only knew what you've helped me through.

❧

Jenna Mammina - Oakland, CA

I've been a fan of James Taylor since I was 6 years old. The first time I saw him in concert was at Circle Star Theater in Merrillville, Indiana, when I was 12. Since then, I've seen him perform at least fifteen more times.

I am a vocalist and songwriter. I've have recorded eleven albums, nine of them with James Taylor songs on them. His music heals me to the core of my soul.

In my many years following JT, I also became a fan of his brother, Livingston. I used to see Liv at the Freight and Salvage in Berkeley. One Sunday night he was performing, and during the first set, he mentioned that his brother James might show up. People were so excited, and every time the door creaked open, I looked over to see if it was him.

At one point I saw a tall man at the door bending down to pay for himself and one other person. I recognized immediately that it was James and Peter Asher! They walked in and sat down three seats away from me.

Livingston knew what a fan I was. At the intermission, he said, "Jenna, I would like to introduce you to my brother, James." At first, I couldn't even talk. I was beyond starstruck. It was James Taylor, and he was shaking my hand.

"Hiiiiiiiii," I said. Then I took a deep breath and continued: "Thank you for writing and playing songs that heal my heart." Although I didn't tell him, I was referring to one song in particular: "Like Everyone She Knows."

James held my hand a little tighter and said, "Keep singing and feeling, it all will make sense in the end."

Afterward, I was invited backstage where a photographer asked if I would like to have a photo with James. Twenty seconds later the flash went off, and I was in music heaven. Then I sat down next to Peter Asher and we started talking about Berkeley and good places to eat. I gave him my handmade business card—my sister and I had made twenty-five the night before, and Peter received the first.

By that time, it was midnight in California, and 3:00 a.m. in Michigan, but I knew I needed to call my brother. When he picked up the phone, I said "Guess who I just met?"

"James Taylor," he said. He knew there would be no other person I would be so excited to tell him about.

The next day I walked in the door of my home and saw there was a message on my machine. I played it: "Hello Jenna, this is Peter Asher. We met last night at the Freight and Salvage with James Taylor. I'm calling to let you know that there are two tickets for tonight's concert at the Concorde Pavilion. Please be my guest and enjoy the concert."

It was 6:00 p.m., and the concert started in an hour. I called my friend Laura and asked: "Do you like James Taylor?"

She answered, "Like? I LOVE JAMES TAYLOR!"

One hour later we were sitting front row center.

For days afterward, I was floating on air.

The following Saturday night, I was telling the story at my gig. As I got to the end of the story, a man walked up to stage and handed me a paper bag with an envelope in it. I opened it, and guess what it was?

The photograph of James Taylor and me at the Freight and Salvage.

I was 25 years old at the time, and I had no idea that James' music would still be healing me today.

CHAPTER 14

Long Ago and Far Away

Martha Reynolds - West Warwick, RI

The first vinyl album I ever owned was *Mud Slide Slim*, which I purchased right after my thirteenth birthday in July 1971, a few months after it was released.

James Taylor spoke to my teenage angst and feeling of not belonging, and I could sit for hours playing the record and reading the included lyrics. Within a short period of time, I'd memorized every word to every song. I knew the sequence of the songs and loved them all.

But one song spoke to me more than all the rest. It was the fourth song on the flip side of the record, "Long Ago And Far Away." With Joni Mitchell singing backup, it became my favorite, and I'd play it over and over. "Why is this song so sad? Why was I so sad?"

I started writing books in my fifties, and my fourth book featured a young woman who had had a great deal of trauma in her younger years, especially during her teens. She used that song to cope, remembering it as a song her mother sang to comfort her as a child. And while I never used the lyrics in the book, I wanted to find a way to acknowledge James Taylor's "Long Ago And Far Away."

After a lot of thought, I decided to call the book *Bits of Broken Glass*, because those four words are in the lyrics and the broken glass is a metaphor throughout the book.

Shortly after the book was published, a friend gave me tickets to see JT at Mohegan Sun in Connecticut. I tucked a copy of the book in my purse, and while my husband and I were waiting to enter the arena, I approached one of JT's "people" and told my story. All I wanted was to give him a copy of the book. He finally agreed to get it to James's assistant. I never did hear anything from James about the book, but I was still happy to have been able to give him a copy. I wanted him to know how he comforted me in my youth, and still does to this day.

CHAPTER 15

Mexico

Steve Oleksiw - Garden City, NY

My two favorite letters of the alphabet: J. T.

In the early 1970s, I went to Camp Hi Rock in the Berkshires for a few weeks every summer. When I turned 16 in 1975, I got a job working at the camp the entire summer. I had the good fortune to work with some great guys who really got me into James Taylor and his music. As a result, I ended up with a ticket to see James at Tanglewood. Yeah!

We arrived early and set up our blankets on the right side of the shed—and as luck would have it, we were close to the bus where James and the band were hanging out. Livingston was sitting next to us. We started talking, and he noticed I was wearing the same clothes as he wore: yellow shirt, brown corduroy pants, and Top Siders on my feet. Of course, he couldn't help but rib me for that.

Soon, out came the frisbee, and we threw for a while, until I decided to make my way over to James' bus. It was still light out, but no one was around. Then, a beautiful woman came out of the bus I knew had to be Carly Simon. "Are you Carly Simon?" I asked. With a half-smile, she responded, "No," and walked away. I knew who she was, but I wasn't going to be a pain.

I went back to Livingston and had a glass of wine with him and the group. Then, I noticed that James was standing on the steps of the bus. Livingston told me to go on over and say hello! I walked over and didn't know exactly what to say. Ultimately, I asked him what he thought of an Ovation guitar (which I had). It was OK, but just OK, he said. I noticed he had a button pinned to his shirt, maybe two inches in diameter, with a picture of the cover of his recent album, *Gorilla*. I wanted it, so I asked: "James, would I be able to have that?" He looked down at it, kinda smiled, and said, "No, no, it's one of a kind." I thanked him, got his autograph on my ticket stub, and listened to another guy ask about the mistake in the beginning of the song "Mexico." I think James acknowledged that it was there. I've tried to listen and see if I could hear anything that was off, but that song is perfect in my ears.

We ended up leaving a note on the windshield of the bus, asking if James would be able to come to Camp Hi Rock and give an impromptu concert for all. That never happened, but I still listened to "Mexico" and the entire *Gorilla* album every day for the rest of the summer. To this day, I still listen to James' music almost daily. I've always said that James' voice is an instrument all to itself. It's just the whole "JT Package." Whether it's with a band, or alone, he strikes something in me that's part of my soul, one which will never grow old or disappear.

When I would play his music for my kids, they would always say, "Not again!" *Yes, again.* Now my kids are in their twenties and they love classic rock, including James Taylor.

I wonder what ever happened to the *Gorilla* button. Does James still have it? I know that if he had given it to me, I would! I have seen James numerous times since that initial concert, and many times at Tanglewood, though I'll never forget that first time.

CHAPTER 16

Moon River

Leslie Buron – Comodoro Rivadavia, Argentina

Cuando era un niño sufria de tartamudez y timidez. Una fono-audiologa me recomendo que aprendiera guitarra y a cantar, que eso me iba a ayudar. asi lo hice y me meti de lleno en la aventura de ser musico.

de esa manera descubri los beatles y una serie de artistas que me tocaban de especial manera, pase mi adolescencia y juventud acompañado de la musica de james, la cual me calmaba e inspiraba. su voz y su impecable fingerpicking, vistieron de magia mis momentos.

y asi paso el tiempo y a los 60 años se me declara la enfermedad de parkinson. la verdad que estoy afrontandola con mucha buena voluntad y estoy muy bien, con mi animo arriba muy comprometido con mi musica, pero obviamente muy atento luchando para estar asi. y es asi que llega a mis manos el ultimo album de James Taylor con canciones como "Moon River" etc y vuelve a acompañarme su melodiosa voz como un amigo que nunca me abandono. quiero agradecerte james por tu arte y tu corazon puestos en cancion.

❦

When I was a child, I was very shy and often stuttered when I spoke. A music teacher suggested that I learn how to play guitar and sing, thinking that might help. Thus began the adventure of becoming a musician.

Soon I discovered the Beatles, and a whole series of artists who spoke to me in a special way. I spent my adolescence accompanied by James Taylor's music, which calmed and inspired me. His voice and impeccable fingerpicking dressed my moments with magic.

At 60, I was diagnosed with Parkinson's disease. The truth is, I am facing it with great goodwill. I am very well, fighting with encouragement from *upstairs* and from my commitment to music. I pass the time listening to beloved artists, and that is how I got the latest James Taylor album with the song "Moon River" into my hands. His melodious voice joins me again, like a friend who never abandoned me.

I want to thank you, James, for your art and your heart put into song.

CHAPTER 17

Mud Slide Slim

Annette Horvath - Davenport, IA

The first time I heard a James Taylor song, I was 8 years old. The year was 1972. My uncles were having a jam session in the garage of my grandma's house, listening to *Mud Slide Slim* and trying to get the songs down. Something in my being said, *That is the most beautiful voice I have ever heard*—James Taylor's—not my uncles'! I felt calm, safe, and mesmerized. I was hooked.

My first JT concert was in 1984 at Palmer Auditorium in Davenport, Iowa, and I went with one the uncles who'd introduced me to James' music. It was an amazing show and I remember crying because I was *there*. I can't even count how many times I have seen James Taylor since. I know that it's been at least thirty. My favorite time was at the Adler Theater in Davenport when he played with his son Ben. It was so intimate, and I was in the front row. I have a purse made from the *Sweet Baby James* vinyl cover, and JT autographed it for me that night.

James Taylor has been a constant in my life, and at whatever stage or event, his music resonates in my heart and soul. I buried my father to James Taylor, gave a eulogy to my best friend with James Taylor, birthed my son while listening to James Taylor, and got married, divorced, and remarried—all with James Taylor's music as a backdrop. "You've Got A Friend" is a theme song for my sisters and me. Every time we are together, that is our jam. I have already laid out for my family the exact James Taylor songs I want played at my funeral, and at what point in the service.

The last time I saw JT was at Wrigley Field in Chicago, and I can't wait for the next time. I believe that James Taylor is a national treasure.

❧

Kay Robinson – Newton Falls, OH

In high school I spent a lot of time at my girlfriend's house listening to music. Her older brother worked at a local radio station and came home with new artist albums all the time. One afternoon, he walked into the living room, handed us an album and said, "This guy will never make it. Here's an album if you want it."

That album was *Mud Slide Slim* by James Taylor.

To be honest, the thing that first piqued our interest was how cute James looked on the album's cover photo. After that day we listened to *Mud Slide Slim* constantly, learning all the words to all the songs; we were both in love!

Imagine our delight when, soon thereafter, we heard James Taylor on the radio. The album from the artist that would "never make it" was released in stores. We bragged to all our friends that we had been fans of his long before he made it big.

The thing that always stood out to me about James' music is his smooth style of singing, the effortless way the music seems to roll out of his mouth, as natural and easy as breathing. His music soothes me. It makes me smile.

After fifty years, I can still see that album cover photo in my mind's eye whenever I hear him sing. Whatever comes my way—bad day at work, disagreement with my husband, moodiness from the kids, all I need to say is, "Alexa, play James Taylor," and it all melts away.

❧

Kelly Ames Smith - CT

The first time I heard James Taylor sing "Fire And Rain" one summer evening on Shelter Island, I was in the third or fourth grade and I was immediately hooked. After that, I saved my money to buy every album. *Mud Slide Slim* has always been my favorite; I could listen to the instrumentals at the end of that song forever and ever. The song "Hey Mister, That's Me Up On the Jukebox" came with a skip in the groove, and so I learned to sing the skip. I can sing every harmony line to every song on all his records.

Years after that summer on Shelter Island, I worked at Time Inc. near Rockefeller Center. I had heard that James and Carole King were supposed to appear on the "Today" show. I brought both albums with me, hoping to get them signed. James, Carole, and Leland Sklar played live to promote the *Troubadour* Tour. One of the show's assistants brought my records to them and they each signed one for me; it was absolutely wonderful! I still have them framed side by side in my arts and music room.

Sending so much joy to you, James, and wishing you many more *golden moments* to come. *Shine like the sun! You're still a gorilla!*

CHAPTER 18

Music

Marco Dossena – Milan, Italy

I wish I could call myself a friend of James Taylor, but "lifelong fan" might be more accurate.

My first concert was in 1985 at the Teatro Tenda di Lampugnano in Milan. It was the first time James performed in Milan. I attended a ridiculous number of concerts after that one—maybe fifty? My favorite song remains "Music," because I think it summarizes James' talent.

In 2002, while visiting London with my wife, Giò, we decided to go to the Apollo Theatre the day before JT's concert, hoping to catch up with him. I was sitting next to the rear door reading Timothy White's book *James Taylor: His Life and Music* (which I had just purchased an hour before) when my wife said, "Hey, look who's behind you."

James was very kind and let us in for soundcheck. We sat in front of the stage and after a while he asked us if we would like to have dinner with him and the band. Of course, we said yes!

When we sat down, I remember his first question:

"Marco, do you like dogs?"

I was surprised because dogs are my passion, and so we started talking about our common love for dogs. I owned seven

Newfoundlands at the time. I definitely think he distrusts people who don't like dogs—exactly as I do! He asked me for suggestions about a dog who could help defend from the bears that used to visit his garden (the twins were very young at this time). The next day, we were invited to a party after the concert, and I brought two T-shirts for Rufus and Henry with my Newfoundland puppies' picture on them. James liked that a lot.

Two weeks later, James was performing in Milan at the Smeraldo Theatre, and we agreed to meet again. After soundcheck, I was invited to his dressing room and we talked for a while. I had brought my Olson guitar to the concert, and we tried playing together, singing along some lines of "Carolina In My Mind."

I also brought him some presents: cutting boards I carved from an ancient olive tree from Jerusalem. James said, "Marco, you give me so much, and I've got nothing to give back." I answered that his music is the greatest present he could ever give me. And I meant it.

At one point during the concert, he said to the crowd: "Two close friends of mine were just married, so I'd like to dedicate the next song to Giò and Marco." The crowd was looking around to see who those two lucky people were; my wife and I were beaming. The song was "Valentine's Day," and Gio and I will never forget that night.

I had left my guitar in his dressing room, so after the concert

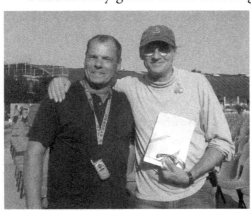

I went back to retrieve it. There I saw that he had signed my guitar and left me the strings he used for the show.

Every time I've been with James Taylor has been a memorable experience. All I can say is: Thank You, James.

◦⁓◦

Noele Martin – San Francisco, CA

What makes a house a home? Family and friends turn a house into a sacred space for making memories and building lives. A home is a sanctuary of growth, love and togetherness.

Like many kids I knew, the houses I grew up in were not safe havens. They had all the appearances of a home: comfortable furnishings and framed family photos on the walls. Sadly, more often than not, my house was a battle zone, the site of much anger, sadness, and suffering.

Even though life in my house was turbulent at best, there was often a lot of music. As a child, music was how I made my great escape. I sang along with the radio, I made up little tunes from books I'd read or movies I'd seen.

Gorilla was the first James Taylor album I heard; I was around 7 or 8 years old. My mother played that album on the living room stereo from time to time. I remember hearing the song "Music." I remember how it felt. Was there really a symphony inside of me?

I was suddenly connected; I heard a voice I recognized even though I had never heard it before. James made it sound like things were going to be all right. My angry little island of pain and fear now had a bridge to another place. This voice told me all kinds of stories, and even though I didn't understand the full meaning of many of them at the time, they felt significant to me.

Suffering speaks unmistakably in music, but so does joy, and I felt all of it. I curled up in that sound and let myself be calmed and centered by it. I felt valued, understood, and comforted. I had found a different sort of home; one with no walls and no roof, yet I still I felt protected. There was someone I could reach out to anytime I needed him. I had a friend.

When I was 10, I was offered the opportunity to join a children's chorus. This would end up having a lifelong impact. I learned to sing in many different languages and eventually joined the chorus's opera company. When I was 11, I took my first trip out of the United States to perform in Denmark. Music became as necessary as food.

Throughout my life, different artists and genres of music have helped me grow beyond and rise above many obstacles in life. Whenever I sing on stage it's a way to connect others with music. I want the music to reach someone the way I was reached. Music saves lives. It definitely saved mine.

James Taylor's music helped me to leave behind the victim. Who I am and who I want to become will be my choice every day of my life. When you realize that who you are can never be taken from you, something beautiful happens. You start to find real freedom. James helped show me where to look.

CHAPTER 19

Never Die Young

Thomas Edwards – Columbia, MO

In 1970, I was 15 years old, hanging out one day with my best bud and cousin, Arturo. He had just bought the *Sweet Baby James* album, and we sat down in his room to listen to it. When the first song came on – "Sweet Baby James" – we were both mesmerized. For me, the song clicked somewhere down deep, and the rest of the album resonated as well. I went out immediately to get my own copy.

I had been playing guitar since 1966, when my sister Kathleen got a cheap Silvertone guitar for Christmas and didn't want it. Just my luck! The Beatles were at their height, and I was 11 years old, in Aurora, Illinois. So, one garage band and much intense learning later, I knew how to play a pretty good chunk of the Beatles' catalogue. When James Taylor came along, I had no idea of his connection to the Beatles, but he was obviously cool, and I wanted badly to figure out his unique guitar style. I worked on the songs as they came along, trying my best to emulate James' voice.

I left home at age 17, moving from Quincy, Illinois, to Montana, to live with a friend from my Aurora garage-band days. We formed a three-piece band and called our band Cordova Spire.

We played church dances and small venues, except for one big festival in Billings—I think it was called Woodstick! About that time, I took out a bank loan and bought a new Martin D-18 for $600. Someone suggested I do a solo gig, so I did, leaning heavily on my JT songs. I played gigs in bars, restaurants, and pizza joints for a few more years.

I saw my first James Taylor concert during the tour for the *Flag* album at the Mississippi River Festival in Edwardsville, Illinois. It was awesome! I've been to several more since, but I think my all-time favorite was in Columbia, Missouri, at the Hearnes Center in 1996. That time I was accompanied by my son, who is named Taylor James.

My wife and I were huge James Taylor fans, and in June 1981, when our son was born, *Dad Loves His Work* was just released. We didn't want to exactly copy JT's name, thus, he became Taylor James and we called him TJ.

Taylor grew up listening to and loving JT too. What a sweet and special boy. He and I were best friends, even though they say you can't, or shouldn't, be "friends" with your kids; something about "tough love," and all that. Not so in our case. At the Hearnes concert, TJ got his first chance to see his namesake, and we had a blast! Though to my everlasting regret, I shushed him during a quiet moment between songs, when he was going to yell out "I was named after you!" I should have let him do it. He and I had many sweet times together, including a road trip from Frisco to Columbia when he was 15, where I let him drive all the way, in my 300ZX.

Sadly, Taylor had a congenital heart defect. It surfaced in late 1998, when he was 17, and he died of pneumonia in the hospital while awaiting a heart transplant. There, I've said it, and it still hurts like all hell. He had a CD of James' *Greatest Hits*, which he played in his car. After his death, I was amazed to see how worn out it was, like he had played it a thousand times. Also, in his last year of high school he wrote an essay about the song "Shed A Little Light," which made me so proud, and he got an "A" on it.

Two of my favorite JT songs are "Walking Man," which I sang to Taylor the moment he was born, and "Never Die Young," which, of course, reminds me of the preciousness of life.

I don't know exactly why JT's music has had such an impact on me, except to guess that he was out there, making these honest artistic expressions about life, at almost every key moment of my life, from age 15 to age 61, and those ripples or waves reached me deeply, as they did so many others, and still do.

From time to time I've thought about how great it would be to meet James, and I know it would be. But as I've aged, I have realized that I already know him in some basic and fundamental way, through his art and the connection to my son.

Thank you, James.

CHAPTER 20

Only A Dream In Rio

Craig Cooper – Sarasota, FL

I know a lot of people say this, but I consider myself the biggest James Taylor fan in the world. From the first time I saw him in 1972 at the Palace Theater in Waterbury, Connecticut, I was hooked. When Carly came on stage to sing "Mockingbird" with him, I was in heaven. I became obsessed with the *Walking Man* album and saw James again at the Yale Bowl in 1974.

In 1975, *Gorilla* changed my life. I hung a picture of James in his white suit on my dorm room door at Georgetown, then purchased my own white linen suit and huaraches. I even grew a mustache like James. Six doors down from my room lived someone who was equally obsessed with JT. In fact, he had the same poster on his door. The two of us became fast friends, and through the years, we've attended many concerts together.

From that point on, I attended five to ten concerts a year. I just couldn't get enough. My first Tanglewood concert was in 1977, and it was like a dream—one I would replay over and over again for the next four decades.

In 1985, after hearing the song "Only A Dream In Rio," I knew I had to go to Rio de Janeiro. I was young and did some stupid stuff while I was there. One night, I found myself in a sleazy hotel bed—one with a radio built into the headboard—next to a beautiful Brazilian woman who didn't speak a word of English. When a JT Live performance came on the radio, I lost all interest in the woman and had to find out where that amazing recording came from. I learned that it was the Rock in Rio concert. I never saw the woman again, but I did buy the tape of that tour, and it was well worth the trip.

I moved to Washington, Connecticut, in 1990. I knew that James had a home in a neighboring town, but I swear that wasn't the reason I moved there. Only in the back of my mind did I hope I would someday run into him. And in fact, I did! One night, my wife, our two-year-old daughter, and I were having dinner at Doc's Restaurant when Livingston Taylor and his wife Maggie walked in and sat at the table next to us. I heard him tell the waiter that his brother would be a few minutes late. I could barely contain my excitement when JT came in. My two-year-old started to throw peas at him, so of course, I went over to the table to apologize. That ended up being a bone of contention in my marriage. My now ex-wife says I encouraged my daughter to throw the peas just so I could speak to James!

I've been to more concerts than I can count, but the most

memorable was a small benefit concert at the Cathedral of St. John The Divine in NYC. I don't remember how I was able to get tickets to this private event, but it was a night I will never forget. My friend was able to record a tape from the soundboard, and it is one of my prized possessions.

Nowadays, I walk five miles every morning listening to my enormous collection of James Taylor music—all of his albums and lots of bootlegs, too. (Remember the days of bootlegs!) I never get tired of him, and I hope he never gets tired of playing for his many fans—of which I wholeheartedly believe I am his biggest in the world.

Dan Mendivil - Lakewood, CA

I began listening to James around 1979/1980 because my older brother was a fan, and of course, it wasn't too long before I became a fan myself. I didn't even have to buy many albums at the time, because I had access to my brother's collection.

The years passed, I grew up, and when James released *That's Why I'm Here* I was completely tuned in again. Each track was a marvel to me, particularly "Only A Dream In Rio." From that point on, I kept an eye on his releases, purchased them the day they came out, and savored each track. Whenever I hear, or even think about a James Taylor song, I'm taken back to a certain period in my life and the memories warm me.

In the early 2000s I finally got a chance to see James at the now defunct Irvine Meadows amphitheater in southern California. The show was magic! He sounded sublime and had a great band with him. I will always be a lifelong fan of his music.

Thank you, James for all that you have done and all that you do.

CHAPTER 21

Only For Me

Curtis Clark – Shenandoah, VA

From the time I was old enough to be swept away by the power of music, to *be somebody else,* that somebody else was James Taylor. My singing voice has a similar timber to James' and his music would often reverberate throughout my body.

As years went on, and I began to understand and desire soul things, more than James' tonal magic echoed in me. His belief in love and our common humanity, and most of all, compassion, have enriched my life more than I can say or know. There is, however, one moment of compassion, only for me, that I do know and want to say.

It was December 2, 2014. James was sitting on the edge of the stage in Baltimore signing autographs during intermission. I had wiggled and pushed my way up to the stage with my James Taylor debut album in hand. I must have pushed too hard, because James gave me a disapproving look. It landed right in the place my dad had forged with

years of disapproving looks. I was in anguish, and James noticed. He autographed my record, and as I was walking away, I heard him say, "Peace, Curtis, my brother."

I didn't turn around, I'm not sure why. Maybe I would have lost it. Maybe I didn't feel deserving. But James' words, a spontaneous wellspring of compassion, have been flowing through my soul ever since.

What a beautiful person. Thank you, James.

CHAPTER 22

Rainy Day Man

Kate Butcher – Kent, United Kingdom

I first heard James Taylor on the radio one Sunday morning in 1964 when I was 16 years old. I lived in Solihull, near Birmingham, England, and music was my main interest. I looked forward to our weekly newspaper, *New Musical Express*, and I began to follow James' career. There was just one record shop in my home village, located above a row of other shops, and I would go there often to browse. The shop had individual booths that we could go into and put headphones on and listen to a track on any album. I spent many hours in that shop listening to both Danny Kortchmar's album, *J is for Jump*, and then *James Taylor and the Original Flying Machine*. The song "Rainy Day Man" was my favorite, and I was a fan from that moment on.

That same record shop had a cardboard cutout of

the picture from the cover of *Mud Slide Slim*, standing three feet by four feet. When they were finished using it for promotions, I asked the owner if I could take it home with me, and luckily, he said yes! I thought I'd never get it in my Austin Mini Cooper, but of course I was determined to make it happen. So, with James and I bent over each other and the stick shift between us, we traveled the whole way home in second gear. I still laugh when I think about that now!

I've been a JT fan since those *Flying Machine* days, and I'm now 71 years old. I live in the south of England, and my daughter, Caelia, lives nearby. A few years ago, James was in Brighton for a concert when Caelia and I happened to be there visiting my son. I was unable to get tickets to that evening's concert, but I asked my daughter if we could take a walk to pass by the venue just to see if anything interesting was going on.

I saw large lorries unloading gear, and just as they were about finished, we crept up to the platform and managed to get in. Just then, Caelia said she needed the loo and needed to find a cafe. She left me on the platform alone, when suddenly, a grill was lowered, leaving roughly a two-foot gap. I was panicking by this time, but thankfully, Caelia came back. She scampered up and joined me. We walked around a little to get our bearings, and to our astonishment, we found we were on the stage!

I waved and bowed to my imaginary fans, then we proceeded further and found stairs and a paper sign that read "James Taylor," along with an arrow pointing upward. A pleasant young man with an American accent approached and said hello. I asked him if JT was up the stairs. He said no; he'd arrive around 4:00 p.m. Next, a jobsworth arrived and was not happy at all to see us. However, he did accompany us to the reception area, where we waited for a few hours to see if we could get a glimpse of James.

My daughter was getting fed up and wanted to leave, but then I looked out the window and saw a tall figure I immediately recognized. It was HIM. He came through the door with another chap and I called out to him. I remembered a lyric in his song, "That's Why I'm Here," about strangers calling him by his name, so out of respect I called him "Mr. Taylor." He must have thought that was funny, and he said I could call him James. I asked if I could take a photo, and he agreed. His assistant also took a picture of me and my daughter with James. I was over the moon! I now have these two photos and they are my prized possessions.

I will remember that day always and will always remain a devoted fan.

CHAPTER 23

Sarah Maria

Sonia Chilton - Richmond, VA

I started listening to James Taylor when I was about 13 years old. Growing up in Richmond, Virginia, he seemed to be everyone's favorite in the late '60s and '70s. Around 1977, my best friend asked me to come to her dorm room at Mary Washington College, because James Taylor had released his best album yet, *Gorilla*. The moment I heard the song "Sarah Maria" I told my friend that if I ever have a daughter, I am going to name her that.

Fast forward to 1985. My first daughter was born—Sarah Maria Chilton.

I am a lifelong fan of James Taylor; he is not only an amazing musician but a wonderful human being.

Thank you, James.

CHAPTER 24

Secret O' Life

Marcia Risner – Nashville, TN

James Taylor has been a part of my life since the early 1970s. My dad was a big fan and often played and sang JT songs for me. I was a daddy's girl, so when my father was killed in a jeep accident in 1971, I was devastated and lost, but I hung on to JT. My brother and I would play and sing his songs over and over, and I fondly recall the two of us singing "Shower The People" as a duet at our church. My brother was killed in an accident in 1988 at the age of 25. It was another tough loss for me, but I carried on our family's love of James Taylor, going to concerts in Nashville as often as I could.

I had four children, and they also became JT fans over the years. At the time of this writing, they are 29, 25, 24, and 20. Through the years I have gone through the pain of divorce, addiction to prescription drugs, and the death of my mom. There were hard times, but JT's songs and lyrics, along with my faith in God, always pulled me through. I found specific JT lyrics for particularly hard times. James and Jesus even got me through the suicide of my husband. Depression followed, and unsubstantiated self-blame ensued. I eventually sought treatment, and I am thankfully on the other side of that now.

James Taylor has been the "house band" for the entire sum of my life. It was enough to finally be on my way.

Then, in 2012 I started feeling very sick; eventually, the diagnosis was liver failure. I learned that I would need a transplant to survive. I never told my kids that I have a rare blood type and that a transplant would most likely never happen. But once again I threw myself into JT's lyrics, and even wrote some of my own. I always fell back on James' story and how he had struggled with a deadly disease of his own: addiction. I recalled the life of his brother Alex and his trials and death. I decided to do all I could to stay alive and do it with a soundtrack. "Line 'Em Up" was a song I had always identified with, because until then I had followed the crowd. But not this time.

I was very sick for a long time. Being on a transplant list should be hopeful, but it is torture. My oldest child, my son, reads me well and perceived what it would take for me to feel happy. So in November of 2014 he brought me to a James Taylor concert in Nashville. It was a struggle. I was weak and sick. I think we both knew it would probably be my last concert. But it was JT, and I was thrilled beyond the sickness. It got me through.

In April of 2015, a 26-year-old woman gained her wings. She lost her life, but she gave me mine—she donated her liver to me.

When I woke up in the ICU at Vanderbilt Hospital in Nashville, I was a new person. I didn't feel sick. I had color in my face, and I felt thankful beyond words. James Taylor's voice streamed through the air like velvet (from a boom box, actually, but as soft as silk). I heard the words to the song "Secret O' Life" about enjoying the passage of time. I live by those words, every day. James says that any fool can do that.

I am doing it.

And now my dream is to meet James Taylor at the next concert I will be blessed to attend.

Patrick Van Wie - Mayville, WI

I heard my first James Taylor song in the fall of 1970 on Milwaukee's AM station WOKY "Mighty 92" when I was 11 years old. Finally, in 1994, I got to see him live at the Bradley Center in Milwaukee. I was in awe to finally be watching this incredible musician perform in person; he is the main reason I picked up a guitar at such a young age. It was a truly emotional experience; his music hits right at my heart.

When I was younger, an older friend of mine who was a Milwaukee musician agreed to help enhance my guitar skills. I showed up to a lesson one day with my JT songbook and played him "Terra Nova." He went wild with excitement at how well I played the song. Then he said, "If you really want to play like James Taylor you need to learn a little more, and you need to learn music theory as well. Guys like him know all that stuff, and I can help you learn it." And so, he did.

Warren taught me how to tackle James' difficult finger and picking style. I'm 58 now and still perfecting getting my strength and coordination in my picking hand as well as finger scales and chord scales. I even learned the "impossible F# (add G#) chord" in "Secret O' Life," the one that stretches over the entire fret board; it's the most beautiful one I know.

Although it's impossible to pick just one favorite song, "Secret O' Life" has always stood out. Not only is it a challenging song to play, it's just so quintessentially James (capo 3rd fret, very fast picking, beautiful cord progression). I still find myself moved to tears when I play it; it's truly food for the soul.

Over time, JT's music has simply become a part of who I am. I listen to and play his music daily. I have my own style of playing and singing, but James Taylor's influence is unquestionably the root of my musical style. He is one of only a few artists that I can listen to over and over and over … it never gets old. In fact, it just keeps inspiring me to enjoy life; his artistry is food for the soul.

103

❧

Amy Wohl – Huntington, NY

During high school, my best friend told me to listen to a song called "The Secret O' Life," by James Taylor. That song was life-changing for me. It tore me down, made me cry, and opened my soul to the truth that I had always felt.

Life wasn't a lovely ride for me at that time, and I needed it to be. James Taylor spoke directly to me. I felt like he was sitting right there on the edge of my bed, his body wrapped around his guitar, and he sang to my needy, painful heart.

He was my handy man; my rainy day man.
He told me to be as I am.
He sang to me in French.
He showered me with love.
He told me to put down what I was doing and climb up the
   stairs to see the stars above up on the roof.
He kicked off his rubber sandals with me when summer
   arrived; MY favorite time of the year.
He sang me a lullaby when I wasn't Daddy's baby.
He walked down that lonesome road with me by my side and
   dried my tears.
I listened to him sing 'til I never knew where the time had gone.
We walked hand in hand, by the edge of the shining sea.
We drifted through time and space.
He held my heart in his hand.

James Taylor does not know me personally, but he has entered deep into the private chambers of my colorful, musical, unconditional loving soul.

And though I've never told him I love him, I do.
Darling, I do.
James, I do love you.

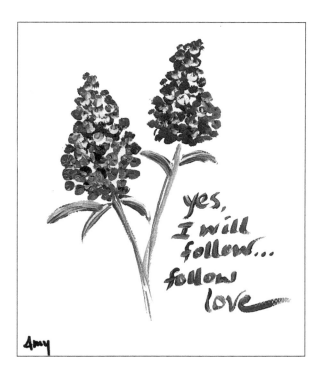

CHAPTER 25

Shower The People

Sharon Baldwin Sittner – Cincinnati, OH

"Do you still suffer from depression?"

That was the presumptive question I asked James Taylor in 2016, one of the several times I've been fortunate enough to speak with him.

We talked briefly about the drug trial I had been participating in for TRP (treatment-resistant depression). I'm not a friend, just one of the millions of fans who has been lucky to grab a few minutes of his time occasionally. He is such a genuinely nice person. He seemed interested and was inquisitive.

Although I didn't recognize it for years, I can now see that the unwavering connection I feel with James Taylor and his music is our shared experience of having to blindly navigate our way through the treacherous depths of major depression. Through the 1970s, I played his songs over and over, clinging to his lyrics as if my life depended on it. And, just maybe, it did.

I don't mean to minimize Mr. Taylor's astounding talents and success by focusing on his bout(s) of depression and addiction, but I do believe it is the common denominator between us. It joins us together (well, at least it joins me to him).

The brilliance of James' lyrics that hint at (and at times scream out) the angst within hooked me from the very beginning. Here was a person who understood my pain even before I could name it myself, a man who was hugely successful despite living with a heaping load of self-destructive melancholy. Of course, I appreciated his smooth voice, his skill on the guitar, his rangy good looks, and his enthusiastic and sometimes impish on-stage performances. But I believe it was our shared pain that grabbed me. And it has never let go.

James "got" me. He hooked me and he understood me, taking his own suffering and turning it into amazing works of art, sometimes deceptively upbeat.

Sometimes I felt he was singing to me, sometimes that he was singing about me. His songs spoke directly to me.

Depression is a strange affliction. It's isolating and guilt-producing. It's often viewed skeptically, as if one is ruining one's life in order to "get attention." It's brutal, and it can be a killer. But the pain is real and it's not a choice.

James spent time in a mental hospital. I have spent time in a hospital psych ward. It sounds scary. It was scary the first time, but I soon realized the people I met there were my peeps. I made friendships I still keep up years afterward. I felt more comfortable with them than people in the "real world."

I feel as if James is one of my peeps, too.

I have trouble feeling happiness. It's not that I don't want to be happy, but rather a chemical imbalance in my brain that makes it difficult for me to experience joy. I'm not just a grumpy, ungrateful, unhappy person, either. It's not a choice I make; it's a truth I have not yet been able to escape. Who would choose to live a joyless life? Not me. And not James!

When I attend a James Taylor concert, sharing a unique experience with my main peep, James Taylor, my other peeps up on the stage, and the thousands of peeps in the audience, I feel not just happiness, but joy!

And I know that things will be much better, if I continue to shower the people I love with love. And that includes James Taylor.

❧

Ellen Emerson-Dyl – Middletown, RI

Many years ago, during a turning point in my life, I saw James Taylor perform at the Newport Music Festival. I was going through a rough time; my husband and I were desperately trying to have a child, to no avail. On the day of the festival, Fort Adams was filled with a sea of people.

James had just started to sing "Shower The People," when he suddenly stopped. He pointed toward the bay and told the crowd to turn around and look up at the sky. We all turned around, and up in the sky was the brightest, biggest, and most beautiful rainbow I had ever seen! There was not one cloud in sight in that beautiful crystal blue sky. The crowd fell silent and James continued to sing "Shower The People."

Everyone got up on their feet, smiling and happy at the awe-inspiring sight we all witnessed, and we all sang along. It was breathtaking and amazing! I hold this memory very close to my heart because at that moment, I knew that everything was going to be just fine.

I was learning to be happy in the moment, no matter what struggles I was dealing with at the time. Life is going to throw things at us, but we can always find the rainbow in the sky.

My husband and I finally had our first baby ten years later, and I recently—at the age of 45—gave birth to our third child.

Java John Goldacker – Merrit Island, FL

Dear James,

I've been a fan since "Fire And Rain" hit the airwaves. In fact, I met and married the love of my life thanks to your music.

I discovered Java the Hut Coffee House because someone told me that a band called Taylor Made played there. The lead singer, Mark, was supposed to sound identical to James Taylor.

Soon after my first visit to see Taylor Made, I got a job at Java the Hut. It was there I met the love of my life, Jennifer, when she showed up one night to see Taylor Made perform.

Jennifer and I married a year later. A month after our wedding, we had the pleasure of seeing you at the King Center for the Performing Arts in Melbourne, Florida. I had drawn a portrait of you, and I asked the theater manager if she could try and get it signed for me. She said it was doubtful, but that she would try during intermission. After intermission, she told us that you loved the drawing and invited us backstage at the end of the show! It was such a pleasure to meet you and get your autograph on the portrait, which I treasure to this day.

Jennifer and I saw you three times together before she passed away on October 1, 2010, after an eight-year battle with cancer. Her favorite song, and now mine too, is "Shower The People."

I will always cher-
ish the memories of my
wife and I attending your
concerts, and I thank you
for *introducing* her to me
through your music.

CHAPTER 26

Something In The Way She Moves

Madonna Busenlehner – Vestavia Hill, AL

Our life with James Taylor began about forty-seven years ago when my husband and I were just two teens in love. His music was a constant with us, whether we were going to dinner or "parking" outside his Dad's house. It's been such an important part of our journey together and never fails to connect us. I would say without question the song that connected us then, and still does today, would be "Something In The Way She Moves."

My husband, Mike, owns an automotive repair shop in Vestavia Hill, Alabama, where Chip Johnson, JT's road manager, gets his car serviced. Over the years, Mike and Chip have talked about how much we love James' music.

Recently, we had the opportunity to be Chip's guests at JT's Pensacola concert. After the show, my husband had the opportunity to show James his battered 8-track tape of *James Taylor's Greatest Hits*.

I think James was just a bit shocked to see that old relic. A smile crept to his face as he listened to Mike tell him how much that old 8-track meant to us. When Mike told James we had been married forty-seven years, he said with a smile, "I wish I could say the same!"

Thank you, James, for being a part of our life together.

Judy Gettelfinger – Sellersburg, IN

I have been in love with James Taylor's music since the first time I heard him in 1970. His music has woven itself into the fabric of my life.

At our wedding in 1972, my husband and I danced to "Something In The Way She Moves." When I was pregnant with my first child, I fell in love with the lullaby James wrote for his own daughter, "Sarah Maria." It wasn't a coincidence that we named our daughter Sara when she was born on March 13, 1976, which just happened to be the day after James' birthday.

My children grew up listening to James in our home; they jokingly call him *Mom's other husband*. Sara went on to have her own musical career in New York on Broadway. Then two more sons, Brian and John, each learned how to play guitar. I'll never forget one show when their band performed "Fire And Rain," and they dedicated it to me.

I've seen James perform in concert at least ten times, even traveling across the country to see him perform with his son Ben, and to pay tribute to my favorite female artist, Joni Mitchel, in LA. On our fifty-second Valentine's Day together, my husband surprised me with tickets to James Taylor's upcoming concert and made sure he got seats close to the stage.

James Taylor's music soothed me when I rocked my children to sleep singing "Sweet Baby James," and now I sing my grandchildren to sleep by singing "You Can Close Your Eyes."

The impact James Taylor's music has had on my life is so special, and now I get to share my love for him with the next generation.

CHAPTER 27

Song For You Far Away

Holly Bond – Nova Scotia, Canada

I was incredibly homesick the first time I heard a James Taylor song in 1986; it was right after I moved to Newfoundland, Canada. Newfoundland is a very rural place, with fishing villages and houses on stilts. I was driving along the ocean and thinking about my parents and friends I had left behind when I moved to this beautiful place. At that moment, "Song For You Far Away" came on the radio. It was the most poignant, beautiful song I had ever heard. I stopped my car and just cried. I will never forget that moment, and from that day on I was hooked on James Taylor.

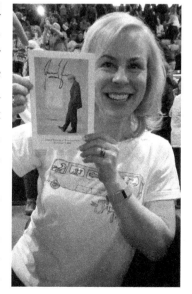

My life has had its ups and downs with long bouts of being ill. I have ulcerative colitis and was very sick from 1990 to 1995. During that time, my mother was dying of lung cancer, and my father soon followed. I had a pulmonary embolism and a divorce a few years later.

I played JT's music when I was alone in my hospital room for a month waiting to find out what was wrong with me. When I was afraid, James' music brought a calm to my mind. When I felt lonely when my mom and dad were dying, I played his music, and we sang along to it together. During my divorce, his music gave me hope, and even helped my ex-husband and I work together in a caring and loving way. We both love his music, and it helped to guide us to be kind to each other.

In 2005, I attended my first JT concert at Tanglewood. I have never been so excited for an event. We went early and we sat outside the fence. James came on to the stage for a sound check, and when I heard his voice, I actually cried with excitement. I couldn't see him, but I knew he was on the other side of the fence! The concert was an incredible experience. Now we drive to Tanglewood every year from Nova Scotia to see him.

I adore James Taylor, and his family, and his music.

CHAPTER 28

Stretch Of The Highway

Paula Hootman – Marietta, GA

James Taylor's music has been the soundtrack of my life. Since 1969 he has been my idol, hero, and a source of great comfort.

In 1996, at the age of 41, I was diagnosed with breast cancer. During my treatment, my husband asked, "What's on your bucket list?" I told him I wanted to see James Taylor in concert one hundred times. Every time I gave JT flowers at the stage and he shook my hand, I felt this charge of energy.

I always told myself, "One more great year is coming." When James gave me a hug after a concert, it counted for five more good years. I would make him baskets and bring them to security in hopes that he would receive them, never really knowing for sure if he got them. I included what I called "James Taylor tea" and "You've Got A Friend cookies" and always a little note saying how much he meant to me.

Another item on my bucket list was to visit France. We went to three different cities on our trip, and I got to see James perform live in all three cities. It was one of the most amazing times in my life. To see him play venues of over a thousand people, with crystal clear sound and a beautiful view of him, I felt like I was being serenaded. Hearing the song "Stretch Of The Highway" portray Chicago while in Bordeaux, France, was amazing. When James smiled at me during the show, a gentleman asked if we were family. My husband just smiled and said, "My wife has a special relationship with him."

Whenever I go to a concert, I want the magic to last forever. I have shared my love of James Taylor with everyone who is important in my life. There is an overwhelming specialness to his music, and I want to share that with everyone I love. I now live in Marietta, Georgia, and have some new friends who, like me, have Taylor fever. I can't wait to sing with them at the next JT concert.

My next show will be my seventy-second, which means I have twenty-eight more shows to go to meet my "hundred shows" goal. James once told me, "Hey, that's good for you and good for me! But what happens when we reach one hundred?" I just smiled and said, "We start over again!"

I had been in remission for twenty-three years, until recently when the cancer snuck back in. But I will not let it get to me. Just like before, it will be a small fork in the road. I still have twenty-eight more James Taylor concerts to see, and when I have a goal, it's hard to keep me down. I am determined and driven and know what I need to accomplish.

And James will be my guiding light.

CHAPTER 29

Suite For 20 G

Dan Holmes – Belvidere, IL

Growing up in the early 70s, I learned to play guitar by listening to the *James Taylor* album released by Apple records, and then *Sweet Baby James*. I had a Harmony Stella guitar that I thought sounded awesome. I ultimately purchased three copies of both of those albums: The first of each was ruined, as I was always in a rush to replay certain sections of a song on my record player so I could imitate and learn the riffs; I bought a second copy to replace the first; and then a third to savor the music.

I adopted a line from "Suite For 20G" as my mantra as I weathered the storms of high school. Someday, I will be free. I still treasure that mantra as a 64-year-old man today. Someday, I will be free.

I have been playing guitar for almost fifty-five years. I am a Christian singer-songwriter with four published CDs, currently looking forward to my fourth tour in the UK. I am still learning James' guitar riffs and songwriting stylings.

Without having been guided by his music throughout my life, I might still be trying to make music with rubber bands and a cigar box!

Thank you, James, for providing a path for me.

CHAPTER 30

Sweet Baby James

Cindy Byers – San Antonio, TX

I can remember where I was and what I was doing when I heard almost every one of James Taylor's songs. And every time I hear a James Taylor song, it takes me right back there! He was (and continues to be) a huge part of my life.

Even more importantly, James Taylor was an even bigger part of my husband, Scott's, life.

Scott was an incredible musician. He had a beautiful voice, and he was an amazing guitar player.  James Taylor was his biggest influence and entire reason for wanting to be a musician. The first time I heard Scott perform "Sweet Baby James" (before we were married) was at a bar in San Antonio. Every hair on my body stood up! I have since found out that is called "frisson," and not

everyone has that reaction. It happens to me with less than a handful of musicians, one being my husband. One of the others, is of course, James Taylor.

In the 1980s, Scott started a band called Blackrose. They became well known around San Antonio and soon became so popular that they started touring throughout Dallas, Austin, Houston, Louisiana, Arkansas, and Oklahoma. They opened for Michael Martin Murphey and Shawn Phillips, among others. They got the attention of Columbia Records, but when they went into the studio to start recording, like so many bands, they argued about creative differences and soon broke up.

Scott went on to play gigs solo and with various musicians. He had a huge following wherever he played. And throughout the years, he continued to play JT's music. He also wrote songs like "Selfish Man" and "Misunderstood" that are very "James Tayloresque."

Scott was a lot like JT, and not just in terms of musical talent. I have always said that if JT hadn't become a musician, he could have definitely been a comedian. Scott also had a great sense of humor; he made me laugh nearly every day of his life.

He played JT's songs (including the lesser known ones) until the day he died of a heart attack on October 1, 2016.

JT made such an impact on my husband and I that we named our daughter Jamie and our son Taylor. Scott used to sing "Sweet Baby James" to our kids every night before bed. When JT came out with a children's book of the same title, I got both Jamie and Taylor a copy for Christmas. It will be a reminder of their dad, and they can read it or sing the song to their children one day.

My love for James Taylor continues to grow, even in Scott's absence. There is nothing like the feeling you get when you are at a JT concert. People of different generations singing along to his songs gives me hope for the world.

I will never hear a James Taylor song without thinking of Scott. Just like JT, he is timeless, and I will love him forever.

❧

Paula Despain – Sandy, UT

Every Saturday morning my children were awakened to JT music playing throughout the house. It was their signal to get up and start helping with the Saturday housecleaning; we cleaned and sang along with James. Both my husband and older son are named James. I've loved James Taylor since the early 70s.

I go to every concert when JT comes to Salt Lake City. In 2001, he came to SLC after 9/11. It was the best concert I've ever been to, and I've been to every concert at that venue since. I wouldn't miss him for the world. At this last show, I screamed like a teenager and got an autograph and a picture with the man himself—what a thrill! I also have a picture with him from the show I attended at the Maverick Center. I had to play the "old woman card" and battle my way to the front of all those crazy fans, but I made it. I love his voice, his story, and his sense of humor!

I guess you could say I'm a 63-year-old groupie!

❧

Laura Hawkins – Gladewater, TX

My son Jacob, "Jake" Hawkins was born on March 1, 1980 with a blood disorder, hemophilia. I was up with him many nights and would sing "Sweet Baby James" to rock him to sleep; changing the lyrics to "Sweet Baby Jake." He loved it; it was our song.

When Jake was 4 years old, he fell and hit his head on the concrete. We took him to the hospital where he was cleared and sent home.

He died later that evening in his sleep.

James Taylor's song has always been my connection to him, and I look forward to the day I go to Heaven so I can sing "Sweet Baby Jake" to my son once again.

Mary Milliman – Sturgis, MI

Over the past year, our family has gone through incredible heartache. Our grandson, Finn Russell, passed away from cardiac arrest eight hours after he entered the world. We were able to hold and rock him during those precious eight hours. Rock-a-bye Sweet Baby Finn.

Listening to James' music has been so incredibly helpful in our healing; his voice has brought peace to our lives in times of heartache. His gentle ways and soothing tone allow us to just sit and listen and get lost in the moment.

Finn was our first grandson; the first child of our son and daughter-in-law. Our son heard lots of James Taylor growing up. My husband and I have many of his albums and have seen him in concert a few times. Songs like "Sweet Baby James" and "Don't Let Me Be Lonely Tonight" inspire us to keep Finn in our hearts day and night.

I hope James knows how much his music and his kind soul help people heal.

❧

Peggi Lee Parker-Butler – Suffolk, VA

James Taylor sings my life story with each song. I find a line, or even a word, that I feel is mine. I've been a James Taylor fan since the beginning of his career. So when I started attending his concerts and saw others meeting him, I wanted to do that too.

It took many years, but I finally got my opportunity on August 17, 2006. James was the very first performer to appear at the new John Paul Jones Arena in Charlottesville, Virginia. At intermission, I made my way down to the stage with two albums in my hands. I stood right in front of JT's mic and waited. He walked onto the stage, right up to me, then knelt, and started chatting with me and signed my albums. I told him I was also going to be at his show the next night in Norfolk, Virginia. He smiled and said, "I'll see you again tomorrow!" I was on cloud nine and floated home for the three-hour drive.

The next day, I had the photo of JT and me from the Charlottesville show enlarged. I took it with me to the Norfolk show. At intermission, I tried to get to the stage, but security would not let me through. I walked around to the other side of the stage and I showed the photo to one of the guards and told him James was expecting me. He smiled and let me through. Just as I got to the stage, James started walking back to exit. I started screaming, "James! It's me, I'm here!" He turned around and recognized me. Then, he walked up and knelt to say he was sorry, but he didn't have a pen. But I had one! As I passed him the photo, it slipped from his hand and floated to the floor, winding its way under the stage. We both were in shock, and JT told security to get the photo. Security dived under the stage, retrieved it, dusted it off, and handed it to James, who proceeded to sign it. People around us applauded!

James is so wonderful to talk to; he likes to ask his fans questions about *us* instead of talking about himself. He once asked me where I was from. I told him Suffolk, Virginia, and that I was one of the first women DJs to play rock and roll music on the radio back in the 70s. There were women on radio, but they were playing elevator music! I had to fight my way in, fight for promotions, and then fight to keep my job—all while working for very little money. I once got in trouble for playing too many James Taylor songs. I told James about this and he laughed and laughed. Here I was wanting to ask James questions, and he was asking me all sorts of things. How can you not fall in love with him?

I had another memorable meeting with JT in Norfolk, Virginia, on March 29, 2011. I had created a carousel horse with icons of JT songs around the horse's neck and on the saddle. We had been told to wait in a certain area with the carousel horse. My husband reminded me to stay cool. Soon, I was telling James that it was a hobby of mine to take old, worn children's hobby horses and turn them into works of art. I pointed out that the entire horse represented the song "Sweet Baby James," including the deep green and blue saddle. He then began really looking at it and touching it. "Oh I get it," he said, and began to name each song that the icons represented such as "Suite For 20G," "Mexico," "Fire And Rain," "Carolina In My Mind," etc. He was so complimentary and could not have been more gracious. He signed the horse, "For Peggi, James Taylor ... with love."

"I'm swooning!"

He turned and looked at me.

"Did that actually come out of my mouth?" I asked.

We all laughed, and my husband said, "I'm sorry James, I told her to be cool!"

I told James that if he ever saw the horse for sale online it meant that I was dead because I would treasure it for the rest of my life. It would be prominently displayed in our home.

It's difficult to put into words how much James Taylor means to me. His music touches my soul like no other. He continues to be kind, gracious, and caring. His band is perfection, and you can tell how much work has gone into making each show a success, even

though it always looks effortless. A night with JT's music is never forgotten. He continues to bring his fans joy, and each song feels like he's singing to each of us individually.

Now friends and visitors come to our home and love to pose with the famous JT horse. Everyone loves James Taylor, Renaissance man.

❧

Gabby Remark – Wilmington, CA

I have been a James Taylor fan for nearly four decades, ever since my friend Char introduced me to his music when I was 16 years old. We would sneak into her older sister's room to listen to JT on her vinyl records.

I grew up and married Char's older brother, Fred. A few years after we married, we tragically learned our first baby was stillborn. When I was delivering him, "Sweet Baby James" was playing on the speakers in the delivery room. I remember laying there thinking, "If this baby is a boy, his name will be James."

Although it was a heartbreaking moment in our lives, that song will always be special to me.

❧

Elizabeth Suh Lane - Kansas City, KS

As a young violinist, I moved to Bern, Switzerland, after a momentous invitation from the renowned violin teacher Max Rostal to study privately with him in Thun, Switzerland. Part of our agreement was that I was not allowed to work with an ensemble, since I was training with him and practicing to become a soloist. He was 84 years old and selected a handful of pupils from around the world to teach from his chalet in Thun.

It was quite a lonely time in terms of social connection, but I communed profoundly with the beautiful nature of Switzerland and the magnificent alps and went for really long seven-to-ten mile hikes daily with James Taylor on my Walkman. His *Best of JT* album uplifted me and motivated me to continue walking and helped me to appreciate the splendor of the snowy alps and the sheer beauty of where I was living. The song "Sweet Baby James," with its reference to the beautiful Berkshire mountains, was especially meaningful. It reminded me to be in the moment and experience the awe of nature and how fortunate I was to live in Switzerland and study with this violin master.

I still remember JT's cassette tape lying beside Bach's *Goldberg Variations*. Musicians know what a gigantic compliment that is. To this day, I have a deep and loving appreciation for JT and his music. It truly helped me during that time of isolation from the world.

The first time I saw James in concert was in Kansas City, almost two decades after my time in Switzerland. A funny side note: I was invited to be a fellow at Tanglewood for four summers when I was a student, but I couldn't afford to go to JT's July 4th concert, and fellows weren't allowed tickets for sold-out concerts. But four years ago, my husband and I, along with some friends, traveled from KC to Tanglewood for JT's July 4 concert. I finally got to experience him at my favorite music festival in the world!

CHAPTER 31

Teach Me Tonight

Roberto & Luisa Andrade – Azores, Portugal

I'm 56 years old, living in Azores Islands in Portugal, and my youth was filled with James Taylor songs. An older friend, now a friend of thirty years, brought me some James Taylor records, along with other albums from Neil Young and Eric Clapton. During that time, it was very hard to find JT records in Portugal, so I had to implore my pen-pal friends to send me cassette tapes by airmail from the United States.

James' music was one of the first things that I introduced to my now wife. Even now, years later, we are able to connect our most romantic moments with songs like "How Sweet It Is (To Be Loved By You)," "Your Smiling Face," "There We Are," and "You Can Close Your Eyes." When we listen, we are transported to all the beautiful places we used to wander around our island when we were first dating.

Of course, James had to be part of our wedding day, so we recorded a special video to express our love for one another, with his music playing in the background. All our three kids were raised listening to JT. Our summers always had an "official opening" when we all would sing "Summer's Here." That was the day summer really started for us.

In 2009, I heard the news that JT was going on a European tour, and was giving a concert in Cascais, Portugal. I bought a bunch of tickets for our family and my best friend's family, right at the third-row front. When I bought the tickets, I didn't even know if we could take holidays on those dates, but I was too excited! Luckily, everything worked out and we ended up making the two-hour flight to mainland Portugal, where we rented a nine-seater van to go to the concert. My wife and kids made a huge banner and hand-painted a "LOVE JT" T-shirt for each of us.

A few days before, I'd made phone contact with the promoter of the festival. I told them how important it would be for us to meet JT and that we were flying 2,000 miles over the Atlantic to see him. During the concert, we raised the banner and shouted, "Azores love JT!" James looked down from the stage and asked, "May I have that at the end?" At the end of the concert, we were able to have a few minutes with James, and handed him our banner. He took

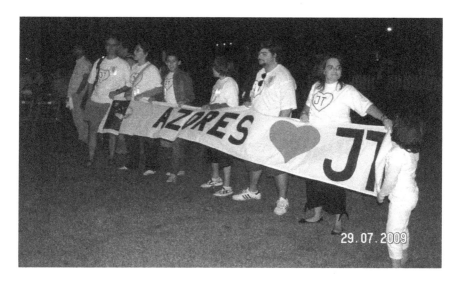

some pictures and signed an autograph for us. Even though he must have been exhausted just having finished the concert, he asked us questions about ourselves and what it was like to live in the Azores.

About two weeks ago, I was told I needed to undergo urgent coronary surgery, something I was not expecting. There was a big wave of all kinds of sensations and feelings. Right at the same time, James Taylor released his new *American Standard* album. During that time of anxiety and preparation for my surgery, my wife and I played that album nonstop. I believe some of those songs helped to strengthen our already rock solid love of thirty-two years. As we listened to "Teach Me Tonight," we cried and held each other and exchanged our vows one more time, both praying it would not be our last.

I'm now recovering from my surgery, so I have nothing but time to go over all the vinyl albums and CDs I have in my collection. I'm looking forward to it. James has a unique way of putting love, calm, and joy into the songs he performs and arranges. The world would be a better place with more James Taylors.

CHAPTER 32

That Lonesome Road

Sharon Baldwin Sittner – Cincinnati, OH

On September 7, 2013, James Taylor was scheduled to perform a special concert at the Salt Lake City Tabernacle with the Utah Symphony Orchestra and the Mormon Tabernacle Choir. Because most tickets were distributed to members of the Mormon church, there was no public ticket sale. Instead, James Taylor's organization had a contest with a drawing for the available tickets. Of course I entered, even though it would mean flying from my home in Cincinnati to Salt Lake City.

I've been a huge James Taylor fan for years and years—since the beginning. I've met him and spoken with him a number of times. In fact, when I went to Las Vegas to see him last year, he gave me a hug and said, "Sharon! I'm glad you could make it." He recognized me and remembered my name!

So in 2013, I started watching airfares between Cincinnati and Salt Lake City, hoping my name would be chosen to receive tickets. Each day, I anxiously checked the mail, hoping to get a postcard informing me that I had won a pair of tickets. Each day, I was disappointed.

I'm not a wealthy person, and air prices were going up as the date neared. Finally, I made contact with James' personal assistant. She responded to my e-mail with a phone call and told me to go ahead and buy my airline tickets, then wait two weeks. If I had not received news that I had won tickets, I was to call her, and she would see that I received two tickets! But she warned me rather sternly that if I *did* win tickets, I was not to call her. I can't believe I was bold enough to ask if I might be able to get *three* tickets, but she agreed. Then, since I have been able to get my picture taken with James, one way or another, every time I saw him, I was even bolder. The conversation went something like this:

I said, "Oh, and also, I pride myself on getting my picture taken with James every time I see him. My friends have come to expect it. Is there any way I could get just five minutes of James's time in Salt Lake City?"

"I'm sorry," she replied, "but James has many commitments on this trip and will not be able to see fans."

"But it's kind of a thing with me. I always manage to get my picture taken with him. Three minutes? Just *three* minutes?"

"No, I'm sorry. James is going to be very busy," she repeated.

"One minute? Just one picture. My friends will be expecting to see one. Just *one* minute?"

"No, it's not possible," she insisted. "But I hope you enjoy the concert. You should get your tickets in the mail within a few days."

Hmm.

I flew into Salt Lake City the night before the concert. The next morning, I was up early, eager to spend the day trying to find James in order to get my picture. By attending many other concerts, I had learned the normal timeline of a concert day for him.

It was hot that day, in the upper 90s, and windy, too. I traipsed around the downtown area, the Tabernacle, and other places I thought James might be. No luck. I knew he and the band usually arrived at a venue around 3:00 pm. So, at three o'clock, I was standing outside the underground loading dock at the Tabernacle, thinking his tour bus would pull in there. I was out on the sidewalk, but when the workers inside saw me keeping an eye on them, they closed the huge garage door.

I decided James *et al.* must already be in the Tabernacle. To say I was discouraged would be an understatement. I had usually been able to find him and get the picture that I was coveting. But now I was hot, sweaty, exhausted, and windblown—ready to return to my hotel and take a nice, cool shower, rest, get something to eat, and ready myself for the night's performance.

My hotel was right across the street from Temple Square, a gated area in the center of Salt Lake City with many attractions relating to Mormon heritage and beliefs. I decided to stroll through and soak up a little of Salt Lake City's culture before going to my room. As I entered, I caught sight of Michael Landau and Jimmy Johnson (both guitarists in the James Taylor band) going up the steps to a small chapel-like building made of stone. Oh, my gosh! I had given up looking for James, thinking he was probably already in the Tabernacle, but if Michael and Jimmy were here, maybe James was, too!

Just before they went in the door, I called out: "Hey guys!" They stopped and turned. "Where's James?"

Jimmy shrugged. "Oh, he's around here somewhere," he said, and the two entered the stone chapel with the red door.

I looked around. There was an information stand behind me. I walked over and inquired about the chapel and what might be going on inside.

The young girl answered, "Probably an organ concert. I think it's private."

Ah! If Michael and Jimmy were going to an organ concert, James must also be there. Outside the open gate, I saw two nice cars parked. I don't know cars, but they were nice, and they were waiting, I guessed, to whisk James and his group off when the concert was over.

A large tour bus pulled up behind the cars, and the busload of Japanese tourists filed out for an hour of sightseeing in the square. When the bus was empty, the driver loped out and sat under the shade of a tree on the grassy area between the street and the sidewalk. From that position, I would be able to see if my hunch was right—if, after the concert, James and his entourage would pass through the gate to reach the two cars. I asked the bus driver if I could sit down with him. He was a tall guy, wearing cowboy boots and a cowboy hat. I remember him chewing on a piece of straw, but maybe I've embellished my own memory. Anyway, he and I sat and had a nice conversation for about an hour. He was Mormon, from Salt Lake City, and he had interesting stories to share. I was still hot, sweaty, and windblown. When his passengers began returning to the bus, he rose.

"Nice talking with you," he said. "I hope you get your picture with James."

And not five minutes later, I looked up and saw a couple of James' band members strolling out the gate, headed for the cars that had been waiting. I got up, wiping the grass from the back of my jeans. I walked toward the gate, and there he was!

"Mr. Taylor," I said, offering my hand, shaking his.

I don't remember what I said. Probably the same inane things I had said in the past: "I'm your biggest fan in the world" … "You are such a brilliant musician" … "You tell the story of our generation."

As always, he was friendly and welcoming. He hugged me, and, of course, I asked if I could get a picture with him. I had my phone out. James looked around to find someone to take the picture. There was a man with him I didn't recognize, but he was willing to take the pictures. He took two pictures. In the first one, we're side by side, James's arm draped over my shoulders, my arm around his waist. After that, I said, "One time when I gave you flowers during a performance, you kissed my hand."

"Well, OK," he replied. "Let's get a picture of that." And we did! I didn't even think of how I looked after hours of wandering around the city in the extreme heat and wind. My hair shows it, but still, I treasure those photos.

From the car, I heard a woman's voice call my name. "Sharon!" she said. I turned to look. Oops! It was James's personal assistant, who I had asked for a few minutes of James's time, and had firmly refused!

"I see you got you the tickets," she said.

"Yes," I answered. "Thank you." I wanted to say, "And I got my picture with James, too," but I didn't want to make her upset. So I quickly went back to the hotel to get ready for the show.

The concert was more amazing than I had imagined; it was different from his typical concerts, of course, but absolutely beautiful. When James sang "That Lonesome Road" (one of my favorite JT songs) accompanied by both the full Mormon Tabernacle Choir and the Utah Symphony Orchestra behind him, it sent chills down my spine. It was so moving.

My whole James Taylor adventure had been well worth it! Thank you, James!

CHAPTER 33

That's Why I'm Here

Fabio Dalla Giovanna – Milan, Italy

I have been a great fan of James Taylor since I was 20 years old, when a musician friend introduced me to his songs with some of his sheet music. When I heard James' music, I started to appreciate the songs and the special way he plays the guitar. I bought all his albums and all the music sheets I was able to find. I attended all his concerts in Italy, and few years ago, I started to bring my son Luca with me.

During a concert break in Milan in 2015, James dedicated his time to signing autographs for all the fans. I approached him with a small acoustic guitar case (8 inches long) I had bought some years before and a gold felt tip pen. Hundreds of other fans were waiting for autographs, but James still took the time to sign the guitar case. When he finished, he told me, "Sorry, this is the best I can do." I

smiled and I thanked him for his effort. It is a treasure I hold dear to this day.

Most recently, I saw James play at the most beautiful concert location in Italy, Terme di Caracalla in Rome. Amazing location and wonderful concert!

I still play his songs almost every day. I was also able to find a clone of James Taylor's Olson guitar in the UK, and it's now my favorite one. It's a cedar top and Indian rosewood back and side. I'm still trying to perfect that James Taylor sound, although I doubt it will ever be as delicate and PERFECT.

Diane Freer – Corona, CA

Back in 1992, James Taylor played the Pacific Amphitheater in Costa Mesa, California. I was working in the box office and asked one of our runners to ask James for an autograph; I was a huge

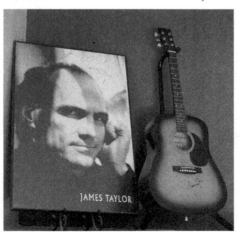

fan. After the show, the runner came into the box office with a giant poster signed by James. Apparently he thought I deserved something more than just a scrap of paper and sent one of his people out to his tour bus for the poster. It's still in my bedroom today, almost thirty years later!

Thank you, James.

Tiffany M. - Newport, RI

I have been to over thirty James Taylor shows and have loved his music for over twenty-five years. I am always plotting how to get closer to the stage; my family jokes that JT probably has a restraining order out against me. Every show I see gets better and better.

Recently, I went to a private event in Newport, RI, where James was the star guest performer. Obviously, I couldn't have been more excited. The opportunity to see one of my idols in such a small, private setting was amazing. I ended up right up front, where I like to be, but as the show progressed, I realized I had to pee! How would I get back up front if I left to go to the bathroom? I wasn't about to risk losing my spot, so I decided to hold it. Anyone who knows me, knows this isn't my strong suit. Toward the end of the show, I was coveting the set list but the urge to go was getting stronger.

One of the stage workers even promised me he would give me the set list when the show was done, so there was no way I was leaving at this point. Long story short, as a grown adult woman, I peed my pants in order to get the set list. My friends were less than impressed, and to make matters worse, I wasn't even given the list! I'd peed my pants for nothing! Well, except I got to sit front row all night at a James Taylor concert. If that's not true dedication, I don't know what is.

❧

Lloyd Soppe - Ft. Lauderdale, FL

I have been called a nut because I have seen JT, Jamo, Walking Man, Natural Man, Mona's friend, Ting's trainer ... seventy-nine times in fifty years.

The first time I saw him was in 1970. I was 13 years old, and I snuck into his show at the Jabberwocky Club at Syracuse University.

He was there trying out some new songs he was working on. I remember him singing an unfinished version of "Don't Let Me Be Lonely Tonight" and "Brighten Your Night With My Day."

Years later, during the Gorilla tour, I went to nine shows in a row, beginning at Carnegie Hall, where he sang "Mexico" with Crosby, Stills & Nash. At every show after that, I started telling the people sitting around me that I was psychic and could predict what songs James would sing next! During that tour, he entered from underneath the stage in his white Miami Vice suit from the *Gorilla* album cover. No one could believe when I even predicted the entrance!

I finally got a chance to meet him at the Saratoga Performing Arts Center, and I told him all about my fabricated psychic abilities. JT loved it! He asked my name, took a lot of pictures with me, and after the encore he came over to me and said, "Good to meet you, Lloyd!"

What an incredible performer and person. I look forward to show number eighty—hopefully in Tanglewood next year!

Daniel Velázquez – Buenos Aires, Argentina

Dearest James,

I am a stranger, one of the thousands around the world who call you by name and gladly pay good money to hear "Fire And Rain" again and again and again.

I have followed your path since I was 15 years old; your "white album" was foundational to me, and I said to myself, "I have to follow this guy." So, it was—I traveled through your music toward the past and the present. I not only sang your songs but also allowed them to decorate moments of my life over the years. I've heard it said that songs from popular artists become the property of the people despite their copyright. I'm sure you'll agree there's nothing wrong with that.

I last saw you in concert in March of 1994. I had begun to believe that there would no longer be miracles, and then the 2017 show was announced. Of course, the rain had other cursed plans, taking away my joy at seeing you. After several days of disappointment, I could digest the news and realize that it's nothing serious, even for a person who has difficulty accepting some things. Nevertheless, I will continue finding your work over all these years on discs, on your webpage, and thanks to YouTube, where perhaps I'll also learn how to build a mousetrap or bake a cake.

Regarding your promise to come back to Buenos Aires, I ask that you please seek out a theater which is not in the open air. Then, maybe I can shake your hand, dear James.

As always with love, support, loyalty, and much affection.

Beth Gibbs – Windsor, CT

In my book, *Enlighten Up! The Five Layers of Self-Awareness*, I devote one essay to how physical grace affects others, and it reminded me of James Taylor. But first, a little background.

Recently, while driving to a friend's house for dinner, I coasted to a stop behind a long line of cars at a traffic light. I felt irritated that I would probably have to wait for two light changes before I could drive on. Off to my left, I saw a woman dancing along the sidewalk to music only she could hear through her ear buds. She stepped off the curb and danced across the street, never missing a beat. Her movements brought a smile to my face. I nodded my head to the music I felt but couldn't hear. My energy shifted as I watched her, and the moment was transformed.

Watching this woman and feeling how it affected me reminded me of a similar experience I'd had a few years ago at a James Taylor concert at Tanglewood. My friends and I had lawn tickets on that sunny afternoon. James was playing and singing, and I stood up to dance. I danced and swayed through the entire concert. I did it because the music moved me, and in that setting no one thinks it's strange to see a woman dancing alone. As my friends and I were packing up our picnic baskets to leave, a man came up to tell me that watching me dance had made his day!

Physical grace can and does have an impact on others. If we develop our personal style of physical grace, we can express it in how we move, dress, walk and dance as we age. This leads to finding and expressing our talent and creativity. James Taylor has clearly found his, and genuinely shares it with all of us. For that, I am deeply grateful. Thank you, James.

CHAPTER 34

The Blues Is Just A Bad Dream

Tom Hunt - Clayton, NY

first heard James Taylor's debut album in 1968 when I was 11 years old. The song "The Blues Is Just A Bad Dream" inspired me to write poetry, and I have continued ever since. Thirteen years later, in February 1981 at a college in upstate New York, I saw James Taylor in concert for the first time. I walked out of the show that night and sat down and wrote this song:

"Play for Me," by Tom Hunt, 02/18/1981

It was a cold night in February
When my dream finally came true
Well thirteen years
Of listening and loving
the steam rolling blues

Now he's finally standing before me
Lookin' a lot like a star
His voice rings out his words to me
as he finger picks his guitar

Oh JT won't you play for me yeah
Play me a tune
'bout your silver moons (chorus)
and your fire and rain
and your sweet baby James
Won't you play for me

Now all these fools around me
they don't understand the man
Who's lived his life
through his words
and all across this land
Now I'm not saying I know him
No, I never did say hello
but I think to myself
I do believe
I've watched the walkin' man grow

Now when I'm feelin' lonesome
or when I want to be someone else
I think of a tune
that JT would play
and you know it really helps
For all his golden moments
keep ringing in my ears
Taking me back
to faces I've known
and the memories of the years

Now you can be Captain Jim
or you're Mud Slide Slim
Sing your highway song
or your Daddy's all gone
but just play one more for me
C'mon now, JT

Without the inspiration of James Taylor, I would have never published my first book of poetry.

Thank you, James.

CHAPTER 35

There We Are

Donna O'Day - Peoria, IL

My friends call me a James Taylor stalker, but I say I just love JT. It is true that I love him so much that I've seen him in concert around fifty times. It is true that when I go to concerts, I'm always sure to make a plan to get a picture or autograph or just a quick hello. It is true that I play his music when I'm happy, sad, scared, or feeling any number of ways. It is true that I can come up with a line from a JT song to apply to almost any situation. And it is true that even though I've imagined many times that his lyrics were written solely for me, I take comfort and joy in knowing that the words indeed meant something to him first.

My love for James Taylor and his music began for me as when I was a teen. It was the late 70s. I was moody and broody, and of course, there was a boy. The first song to wrench my guts was "There We Are," which I played while things were good, and more often when things were not so good—it was a great song for crying my eyes out. Luckily, I moved on to happier and more hopeful messages, so that when I went to my first JT concert on my twentieth birthday on July 5, 1979, at the Mississippi River Festival in Edwardsville, Illinois, I was sold on "Your Smiling Face" and "Secret O' Life."

Through the years, I continued to love James and his music, but didn't reconnect with his concerts until the 90s, when I tried to attend a show anytime he played nearby. I live in Peoria, Illinois, so most often that meant traveling to St. Louis or Chicago. He played in Peoria a few times, which is always a thrill, sort of like inviting him over. As I mentioned, I always like to grab a picture or autograph and have often spoken with him at intermission or after the show. Friends ask all the time if he recognizes me because I've been able to meet him so many times. While I'd like to think that is the case, I tell my friends that he is so very humble and kind, that when he talks to me or to anyone else, it's like talking to an old friend.

I have many JT "stories," because every concert or event involves so much planning and attending and sharing the love with special friends. I will always remember my first concert; the first time I met him; the Troubadour reunion; the ballpark concerts; my trip to Tanglewood; or the time back-up singer Arnold McCuller took my phone around the stage during "How Sweet It Is (To Be Loved By You)."

However, I do have both a fun story and an all-time special moment.

First, the fun. A few years ago, JT did a short tour with his son Ben. We saw them in Moline, Illinois, and after the concert we talked to them at the stage door. We headed home—about a two-hour drive—and stopped around midnight in the middle of nowhere to use the restroom. We were the only ones in the gas station, or so we thought.

We came out of the restroom and JT, Ben, and a few of the band members were loading up on road supplies. We chatted with JT again, and he said, "Didn't I just see you in the alley?" We invited him to follow us home for breakfast, but he was headed to another venue. My husband always refers to this as "the time you stalked JT at the gas station," but I remind him that we were there first, so surely JT was stalking me!

But my all-time special moment has to be the one I experienced in February of 2018. When I learned last summer that JT would be receiving the Kennedy Center Honors award, I felt compelled to go to the performance event in Washington, D.C. I quickly learned that getting tickets was very challenging, and I found myself on a wait list for about a month prior to the event. I flew to Washington with a best friend and devoted JT fan. We were notified literally two hours prior to the show that we had secured tickets. I like to think that in some small way, I helped represent the everyday fans that JT cares so much about. Similarly, I like to think that we were being honored as well for relationships that have spanned the decades.

I'll wrap up by saying that without a doubt, James Taylor's music and presence has had an impact on me. As one who seeks meaning and inspiration from all around me, I find that his music and lyrics have often been the source of my comfort, my solace, my inspiration, my energy and my love. He writes about feelings and ideas and connections that I need in order to acknowledge my past, to be at peace with my present, and to remain hopeful for my future.

I keep all of James Taylor's music in my heart and in my soul, always.

CHAPTER 36

Today Today Today

Kim Lifton - Farmington Hills, MI

had been divorced for a year, and I was ready for an adventure. So, when Rebecca Gold, a James Taylor fan I met on Facebook, invited me to see a JT concert with her, I said "Yes!"

She invited me to her home in Providence, Rhode Island; we would go to the James Taylor/Jackson Browne show at Fenway Park in Boston.

Rebecca first reached out to me in May 2016, a day after I posted photos online from a James Taylor concert in Toledo, Ohio.

"Hi Kim!! I love your posts and pictures from the James Taylor concert last night!" she wrote. "Can I share them on my JT fan Facebook page: *Life with James Taylor*?"

"Of course!" I replied.

Immediately, I could feel myself being pulled toward Rebecca; it was as if I knew her, but I did not. Not beyond social media. We were both writers and journalists. We were born a week apart in 1961 and shared the Cancer astrology sign. And we had both been to sixty or more James Taylor concerts. I was intrigued.

For the next few weeks, logging onto Facebook and looking for a message from Rebecca became a highlight. She was working on a book about her connection to JT's music. I could relate. She said he saved her life during some major challenges when she was a teenager. Me, too.

It didn't take long for the concert invite. She was going to three JT concerts over the summer in Chicago, Boston, and Tanglewood.

"You're crazier than I am," I wrote.

After we made plans to see the Boston show, I briefly wondered if my new friend might be cuckoo. Or even worse, a stalker! But somehow, I knew that Rebecca was just a middle-aged woman who, like me, shared a genuine love for James Taylor.

A concert with another super fan had to be more fun than my post-divorce life, which wasn't what I had expected after ending an eighteen-year marriage to a man who cheated on me. James Taylor had never disappointed me.

A few days after my husband moved out, I went to a James Taylor concert (July 2014), where I listened intently to the words of each song, searching for strength to get through the divorce. His first song was new: "Today Today Today." I thought he'd written it for me.

Later that night, as James began "You've Got A Friend," I started fussing with my wedding band, holding it, twisting it, staring at it. I was afraid to take it off because my daughter was out of town and did not yet know her dad had moved out. I wanted to tell her before doing anything. But as James sang about people hurting you and deserting you, I placed my index finger and thumb on that ring and slipped it off, effortlessly. I sighed.

I listened to James' music nonstop for months during the divorce process. I didn't do anything too wild, though I had a few memorable encounters, like downing half a bottle of twenty-one-year-old single-malt scotch that was gifted to my friend for his birthday; hosting parties for a bunch of married moms who came to my place after work to drink, eat their marijuana-infused edibles, and watch "The Girlfriends' Guide to Divorce." The house I shared with my 16-year-old daughter became a temporary sorority house for middle-aged moms.

I was excited to catch a James Taylor show at Fenway Park with Rebecca. We continued chatting for months. We talked a lot. Phone. Text. Facebook. Email. About James. My ex. Our kids. Our moms. Her husband. About the blind date with a guy named Steve (who is now my boyfriend!) I'd had a few weeks before.

Rebecca told me James saved her life through his music during high school. I told her my connection began in 1978 when I, too, was in high school. My best friend, whose name was Jim, introduced me to JT's music. Jim was editor-in-chief of our school newspaper; I was the features editor. I nicknamed Jim "Sweet Baby James." Once, he bought me a dozen individually wrapped red roses from the student council on Valentine's Day; he also left two unwrapped books of sheet music on my desk inside our school's journalism classroom. One was *JT*, his eighth album, which had been released the previous spring; the other was *Sweet Baby James*.

We played James Taylor's music in our newsroom while we pieced together the newspaper on light tables and edited with X-acto knives. I can still see Jim standing in the middle of the classroom, jamming on an air guitar to "Steamroller Blues."

After school, my twin sister, Hope, and I would squeeze into Jim's maroon two-seater Triumph Spitfire convertible and drive around town with the top down, playing "Sweet Baby James" and other JT tunes so loudly that other cars on the road could hear us through their closed windows.

I fell madly in love with James Taylor, but not with Jim.

Rebecca loved that story. She and I became *instafriends*, like two young elementary schoolgirls who met on the playground during recess and, within a few days, were sharing peanut butter sandwiches, taking turns hosting sleepovers, and walking arm-in-arm on the way to and from school every day.

Even though we had not actually met. I wondered: How could I feel such a strong connection to this person I'd never seen in person? It defied all logic. But Rebecca and I seemed to understand each other. I trusted my gut.

We hugged when she picked me up at the airport, as if we were long lost friends catching up after decades apart. We went to her house, and she gave me a quick tour. The kids' room. Her husband's fancy coffee maker. Her James Taylor album covers. Her office.

The closet door was open when we walked into the master bedroom; I noticed a grey jacket, CAbi brand, made of comfy sweatshirt material. I had that same jacket. Even her clothes looked like mine!

Rebecca and I talked about all the JT concerts we had seen. Tanglewood, in the Berkshires, was our favorite venue. I'd traveled there twice. Once was on my birthday, July 4, 2015 when I drove from Detroit to Lenox with a friend in her light-blue Mini-Cooper. Rebecca went to Tanglewood every summer.

I told her my twin sister, Hope, died when we were 40. James Taylor's voice soothed me for the entire year afterward. I had "Fire And Rain" on autopilot; that song was etched on my mind. I knew he wrote it in a mental hospital. Hope, my twin, was bipolar. I knew James understood despair. Hearing his voice, and songs dealing with struggle, addiction, depression, pain, love and loss comforted me. It's as if he understands me, too.

Rebecca's husband played "Secret O' Life" for us on his acoustic guitar. It's one of her favorite songs, and mine. It reminds me to stay focused on living and moving forward. We talked about the song "Blossom"; it reminds me of Hope, who planted rose bushes outside my parents' front door. When the rose buds blossom, I feel the presence of a young, healthy twin standing beside me, and I can hear James Taylor singing that song inside my head.

Rebecca and I talked about why we love so many of our favorite songs. As a bonus, I went to Rebecca's mother's birthday dinner, helped her son with his college essay, and saw an incredible show at Fenway Park with James Taylor and Jackson Browne. We danced for most of the concert, while others remained seated.

My friendship with Rebecca transcends my love of James Taylor's music. We talk or text several times a week. We sometimes write together on Zoom. Or do online yoga. I attended a wedding last fall in Boston; I flew in a day early just to visit Rebecca.

James Taylor brought us together at a time I did not even know I was looking for a friend.

Thank you, James.

CHAPTER 37

Up On The Roof

Kimberly Benton - Chesapeake, VA

My daughter Taylor, who has cerebral palsy and is confined to a wheelchair, received tickets to a James Taylor concert in Virginia Beach for her fifteenth birthday. She was so excited, and the first thing she said was, "Can I meet him?" I told her that was highly unlikely, but that I would try and see if there was anything I could do.

So, I sent a letter to the Virginia Beach Amphitheater asking them to forward our request letter to James Taylor's staff. I never imagined it would actually get forwarded, but I wanted my daughter to know I tried. Well, the unimaginable happened and James' assistant reached out to us and invited Taylor to the sound check before the concert. The whole night was absolute magic. It was one of the most wonderful and memorable experiences of our lives, especially Taylor's.

When Taylor turned 18, three years after the concert, we found ourselves petitioning the court for guardianship of her. We learned that guardianship hearings exist to ensure that people with disabilities do not lose their rights to self-determination. Before the hearing, a court appointed advocate interviewed Taylor at our home. The

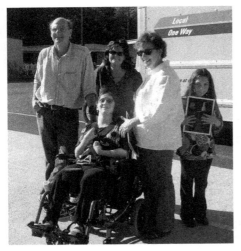

purpose of the interview was to make sure that guardianship was necessary, and she was not being taken advantage of. Taylor's speech was often difficult for strangers to understand, and she rarely spoke to people she'd just met.

I was surprised when Taylor warmed up to the advocate quickly and was very chatty with her. After some assessments and questions regarding Taylor's disability, the advocate asked what she was interested in. Taylor told her how much she loved music. Every time she heard a song new to her she would want to know "Who wrote it, where was it recorded, did anyone else cover it?" She never forgot a single detail.

When the advocate asked who her favorite singer was, Taylor said, "James Taylor!" The advocate was amused and said, "I didn't expect that because you are so young!" Taylor told her all about going to the concert and meeting him. We showed her the scrapbook made by a family friend who went to the concert with us. Taylor showed her the program on her wall that James Taylor had signed for her that night. The advocate said, "I was already a fan of James Taylor, but I became an even bigger one after this story."

On the morning of the hearing we were seated in the back of a packed courtroom. After court was called into session the bailiff approached our attorney and the advocate in the front of the room. Our attorney came to inform us that the judge wanted to see us in his chambers. The attorney indicated that this was very unusual.

While Taylor was cool as a cucumber, we, her parents, were feeling very uneasy.

Inside the chambers we saw Judge Krishner seated at a conference table. After introducing himself, he said, "Taylor, I understand you met James Taylor. I have seen him in concert three times, but I have never met him. That must make you pretty special!" The judge pulled out his iPhone and asked, "What is your favorite JT song?" She said, "'Up On The Roof,' but actually it was written by Carole King."

The judge laughed and played the complete song—to Taylor's delight and everyone else's amazement. When it was done, he played the song "Mexico" and said, "This is my favorite."

Our attorney whispered to us, "This never happens; this is really something."

When "Mexico" was over, the judge announced that guardianship was granted and Taylor is clearly where she needs to be, where she is so well cared for and clearly loved."

We thanked the judge and exited the chambers with the attorney and the advocate. As we rolled her out, Taylor yelled, "Bye Judge, thank you!"

In the hallway outside the courtroom, our attorney said, "Taylor, in all my years of coming to this courthouse I have never seen anything like it, the judge playing music on his iPhone during court! I don't think anyone but you could have made that happen." Taylor smiled like she expected nothing less. The attorney and advocate thanked her for making it such a special day.

Before leaving the courthouse, we had to file the guardianship papers with the court. Our attorney escorted us to the appropriate office and started to tell the clerk what had happened. The clerk said, "I heard! The whole building is talking about it!"

The attorney laughed and said, "See Taylor, I told you this was a big deal!"

This story has proven to be long reaching in our family. Our youngest daughter, Gracie, was only 8 years old when she, too, met James Taylor at the same concert. Years later she was playing guitar in the lobby of her college dorm when a professor known for being quite stern approached her and said he bet she hadn't heard of the kind of music he liked to play. He said he liked to play a lot of James Taylor's music. She replied, "Yes sir, I've met James Taylor," and proceeded to show him pictures on her phone to prove it. He replied, "You can call me David," and shook her hand, much to the astonishment of his teaching assistant, who was with him. As the professor was walking out, the assistant approached Gracie and said, "You're very lucky, I've never seen him like this!"

In May of 2015 Taylor died at home, surrounded by her family. It has been more than five years, and we still grieve her loss daily. Comfort while grieving comes in many forms and they include thinking of beautiful family memories and listening to a lot of James Taylor's music. In the early days after her passing we would say, "Taylor can't be here now, she is "Up On The Roof." One day we will be reunited with her there.

~∽~

Don Corn – Robinson, IL

I first saw James Taylor in 1971. My wife and I are big fans of live music, so we attend several concerts a year. We always look forward to Mr. Taylor's shows; we both love his style and songs.

One concert in particular stands out in my mind. It was at the Murat in Indianapolis in March 2011. This tour was a bit different because James was with his son Ben Taylor. We were able to get front row seats!

My wife is a semi-professional photographer and is usually told at the venue door that she can't bring her camera into the show. But on this evening, they didn't stop her. There we were, sitting a few feet away from one of my heroes, and my wife has this great camera with her.

The first set included some great songs from James and Ben. "Up On The Roof" was a highlight for me, with both James and Ben singing and playing it together. After finishing the set, James put his guitar down and saw me holding up a CD cover and a marker I had brought with me. He asked, "Would you like me to sign that?" He came over and signed my CD cover. I was thrilled. I remembered that the night before he had won a special presidential award, so I congratulated him on it. He said, "Thank you. But I don't want to brag about myself, so let's just keep that between us."

Being a drummer myself, I asked if Chad Wackerman (his drummer on this tour) ever came out after the show to sign or chat with fans. James said, "I'll let Chad know you're looking for him." I figured that was his kind way of brushing off my request.

I had always dreamed of meeting James, but to find out he was such a kind person made it so much cooler. When James moved over to the other side of the stage, I noticed that his son Ben was standing off stage steeping a mug of tea. I caught his eye, held up my CD, and asked if he would sign it. Ben nodded yes. As the second set started, Ben came out and signed one autograph ... mine!

At the end of the second set, the band took their bow and left the stage. After a few minutes, James came back out and shook hands with the fans. Then, to my delight, Chad Wackerman came running out to greet my wife and me. He didn't have much time, but he let us take a photo with him, and he signed my CD cover.

As we walked out of the Murat, my wife wanted to take my photo in front of the marquee. After a few minutes, out came James and Ben. James headed to the crowd and Ben toward the bus. I figured James might be there for a few minutes, so I headed to Ben. I asked for a photo and we chatted for a bit. I told Ben that I loved his latest

CD and he said, "I know; I saw you tonight in the front row. And you and I both know that no one, and I mean NO ONE, came here tonight to see me. They all came to see Dad. But I watched you sing every word to all my songs. You can take as many pictures with me as you want!"

After Ben walked away, I noticed that back-up singer Arnold McCuller had walked onto the bus and was sitting in the driver's seat. I took the opportunity to walk over to the driver side window to see if I could say hello. He opened the window and we chatted for a few minutes. Then he said, "Watch this!" Arnold waited until several fans walking by got directly in front of the bus, then laid on the horn. He did this several more times and we laughed and laughed. It never got old.

With everyone finally on the bus but James, my wife and I went over and waited in line for a few more photos. Finally, it was our turn. James turned and saw it was us. Without hesitation he said, "Oh it's you! Did you get to meet Chad? I can go get him for you!" We assured James that we did, but we were amazed that he remembered.

Getting to meet a hero isn't always what you hope. That was not the case that evening; James was warm and kind and gracious and seemed truly excited to meet with us and his other fans. I will never forget such a fantastic evening. Thank you, James.

Joe Moran – West Seneca, NY

I have been a James Taylor fan since the 1970s, but the first time I saw him perform was at Darien Lake Amusement Park in 2003; I was with my wife, who was also a huge fan. The show was magical. He sang all my favorites with his heart and soul, like he always does. During the song "Up On The Roof," when he sang about the stars lighting up the sky, there was a slight pause, and suddenly—an explosion of fireworks. The band stopped playing, James stopped singing, and we all stood there together watching the sky. It was truly a magical moment I have cherished ever since.

The part of the story I usually hold back is that my wife and I had been trying to have a baby for several years and had gone through several miscarriages, the last being about a year or so before this concert. We had pretty much given up on having children.

Coincidentally, our only daughter, Elizabeth, was born about nine months after that magical night.

⤚⟋⤙

Sandra Perdian - Garrettsville, OH

I know everybody says this, but I really am James Taylor's biggest fan, and have been over a *long* stretch of time. I loved his voice as a teenager, and now that I'm in my sixties, he's still my absolute favorite.

At 16, when I heard the news that James married Carly Simon, I remember thinking, "Shoot! I can't compete with that." Funny what goes through a young girl's mind.

I married at 19, got divorced, and became a single parent by 21. A local farmer agreed to lease the top floor of his farmhouse to my son and me. Every other weekend my son, Scott, visited his dad, which left me all alone in a tiny studio apartment with nothing around but corn fields. I would sit for hours by the open window letting the breeze hit my face while I listened to James Taylor sing "Up On The Roof." It felt like he was singing right to *me*. All his songs lifted my spirts and brought a smile to my face.

I eventually remarried and had three more kiddos. Twelve years into my second marriage, I was told I was "mental" and should seek help. I couldn't hold my coffee cup with one hand because the cup would shake. I vividly remember my heart actually hurt. I began plotting my way out. I had the means to do it and even wrote a goodbye letter to my kids. But a chance encounter with a persistent social worker got me into therapy, and it worked.

My therapist encouraged me to do things that made me feel good. I remembered the farmhouse—when I'd sit in the window and listen to James' music. I can honestly say his songs still bring me joy.

Two years ago, my husband and I were visiting Scott, his wife, and our granddaughter. It came up that James Taylor would be putting on a concert at Blossom Music Center in Ohio that coming summer. I told them that I'd love to go, but I didn't have money for tickets. Scott knew I was down in the dumps about turning 60, and he replied, "Well, your sixtieth birthday is coming up. That might make a good gift, but we can't buy two tickets, only one, and we know you wouldn't go by yourself."

I shouted, "Oh YES I would!"

All four of my children chipped in and bought the best seat available: fourth row!

Prior to the concert, I'd broken my left foot and had to wear a boot-type cast. They are *heavy*. I arrived three hours before the concert, and there were only three cars in the lot—or so I thought. Little did I know that there were multiple lots closer. I had to walk past every single one of them to get to the venue. Blossom Music Center is in a hilly area dense with pine trees.

My seat was amazing, and I loved every minute of the concert. James is such a wonderful performer, and he's quite humorous on stage. I soaked up every minute.

Unfortunately, when the concert came to an end, and it was time to walk back to my car, I had absolutely no idea where I'd parked. I had been so enthralled getting to the concert that I forgot! There were cars everywhere, gridlocked while trying to leave. It took a good hour, but I found my car and just sat inside remembering how wonderful the evening had been.

A few years ago, James posted a photo of himself backstage with a young lady who had Down syndrome. It melted my heart. My brother, who had Down syndrome, died a few years ago. He loved getting backstage to meet celebrities, and the photo reminded me of him.

James' voice is soft and soothing, and his songs are woven into the memories of my life. James and I have been through a lot together, so to speak.

He just feels like home.

CHAPTER 38

You Can Close Your Eyes

Nancy Bisbey – Davenport, IA

I always play James' music to get my kids to bed, singing "You Can Close Your Eyes" as they fall asleep. James has been my salvation, and he will always be my go-to guy when I need something familiar and warm.

My son Alex is autistic and nonverbal, but he knows a James Taylor song when he hears it! In 2010, after sending many emails to James to let him know how much his music means to my family, he invited us all to his concert as his guest. That concert, in Davenport, Iowa, was a night I will never forget. During the break, James and his son Ben came to the edge of the stage to sign autographs and take pictures. James gently laid his hand on Alex's head. Alex may not have known how special this moment was, but Momma sure did.

James Taylor is not only one of my favorite musicians, but he is also one of the kindest and most genuine people out there.

CHAPTER 39

Your Smiling Face

Suzanne Bartley - Manalapan, NJ

Ineffable: Incapable of being expressed in words. When I attempt to put into words how James Taylor has affected my life, ineffable is first thing that comes to mind. How do you capture a soul-to-soul gift in words? How do you aptly describe the tapestry of emotions another human being's musical expression gives you? It is too extraordinary a feeling to be limited to words.

We all have that artist, that special one who you can connect with on a level like no other. Perhaps it's a musician, a painter, dancer, or maybe an author. For me, it is James Taylor. His voice, musicianship, and lyrics are a gift from the soul and received by the soul.

I fell in love with music at an early age. As soon as I was able to operate the stereo on my own, I could be found dancing in the living room to the Beatles.

Then there was the day that my life changed forever. I was 8 years old when I heard the song "Your Smiling Face" by James Taylor. There it was. There he was—the artist who would be there for me for the rest of my life.

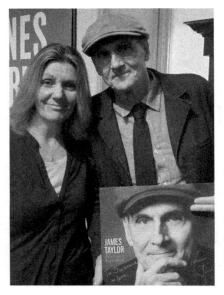

My family moved quite a bit while I was growing up, from Pennsylvania to Minnesota, to New Jersey. It was difficult for me being the new kid so often. For the most part, music is what sustained me. For me, music is oxygen. It is life. I feel beyond blessed to have discovered James Taylor at such a young age. I'm thankful to exist at the same time as this very special man.

My life has been enriched by the beautiful music and messages of James Taylor. I am a better person for letting his music wash over me. His music has helped lift me out of depression. It's motivated me, empowered me and helped me to appreciate and fully live my life.

James' message in "Secret O' Life" is a guide to life. It is one of the most beautiful songs I've ever heard, and it resonates with my soul. It is a song that seems to have come through him from a higher place. I've often heard artists speak about music simply coming to them as if they're a vehicle for a message from the universe. I believe "Secret O' Life" is one of these songs. My children gifted me with an engraved wooden plaque with the quote: "The secret of life is enjoying the passage of time." It hangs over our living room clock and serves as a daily reminder to be mindful and enjoy every moment.

In 2016, I took my daughters to a James Taylor concert at an outdoor venue in Holmdel, New Jersey. All four of my children have grown up with James Taylor and have a deep appreciation for his music. I've no doubt his music will continue to transcend time as the magic of James Taylor is passed through generations. During the intermission, instead of leaving the stage to take a break, James sat down on the edge of the stage and began to greet people. Although we were nineteen rows back, I took a chance and made my way to the front of the stage. I got closer and closer until, before I knew it, there I was! Face-to-face with James. It was quite loud in the venue, but I managed to say, "Thank you." He signed my concert ticket, and I got a photo with him. Emotions took over as I made my way back to my seat and the tears flowed. Happy tears! Here's that word again, ineffable. To adequately describe what this meant to me is beyond my capability.

Recently, I had an experience that was the sweetest, thickest layer of icing on the most glorious cake ever. I learned that James was going to be at the Union Square Barnes and Noble in New York City for a signing of his new album, *American Standard.* Together with my daughter Emily and my son Jay, we boarded the 5:23 a.m. train to NY Penn Station. Upon arriving at the bookstore, we realized we'd made it there early enough and would indeed receive one of the limited number of wristbands. This is when I began to cry for the first time on that wonderful day.

The second time the tears came was when I had the wristband in my hand and knew that in a few hours I would be face-to-face with someone whose existence has made my life journey much better. What would I say? I knew I might freeze, and there was no doubt that whatever I said would be peppered with tears. How do you capture how the music, the expression of his soul, has touched you?

When it was my turn, I felt so fortunate and incredibly blessed as I walked toward this most incredible spirt. I was acutely aware of the moment and what was happening. How rare is it to stand face-to-face with a person who has not only had a positive impact on your life, but also with millions of others worldwide? I was given the chance to directly express to the person who has had such an impact on my life, what he has meant to me.

I brought him a small gift, a plaque that read: "To the world you may be just one person, but to one person, you may be the world." I told him that I hope it may serve as a reminder to him of how special and beloved he is by me, and countless others.

James Taylor's music has been an integral part of the joys, sorrows, challenges, loves, endings and beginnings in my life, including singing and dancing with my newborn to "Your Smiling Face."

Reflecting on what this very special soul has meant to me, reflecting on how to express it, it all comes down to two words. Two words that encapsulate the gift this one soul has given to another soul: Thank you.

∽

DeeDee Narasky – Rohnert Park, CA

My son is 21, autistic, and for the most part, nonverbal. Music has always been a big part of his life. My husband and I enjoy music, and he plays guitar for personal enjoyment. As a result, my living room looks like a music studio. We're 1960 babies, and we really love music from the 60s, 70s, and 80s, so not only does my son hear music of his generation, but he also gets to enjoy our generation's tunes. He's always grabbing my phone, launching iTunes, and listening to music. He has favorites: the Beatles, John Mellencamp, Bryan Adams, Bonnie Rait, and James Taylor. When he's walking

around with my phone in his hand singing the lyrics word-for-word, it melts my heart.

In the spring of 2015, I started following the JT Facebook page just to keep up on current events and find out about tour dates here in California, which are rare. Then, in December 2015, JT posted something about new music, and it just so happened to be the same afternoon my son was singing along to some JT classics!

176

I posted in the comments, something to the effect of "My nonverbal autistic son loves your music, it gets him singing your lyrics and makes this momma proud. Thank you for all the years of music and Happy New Year."

About four hours later, I got a private Facebook message from a woman whose name I didn't know, and I almost ignored it. But I'm glad I opened it: the message was from James' personal assistant. She mentioned James read my post and wanted to offer my son a signed CD. I was elated! During our chat, I said that we'd missed JT's tour here because the show was the same night as my son's high school graduation. She offered her personal email and told me to watch tour dates in our area and to reach out to her if we saw something near us. *Wow!* I thought. *Awesome.*

Over the next few months, as James was releasing dates for the 2016 tour, I saw he was coming to two California venues. The closest was two hours away, but to make a dream come true for my son, we would make the travel arrangements. I sent James' assistant an email in April, a few months after we'd talked. I felt weird, like, *Uh, remember me?* But she was very pleasant. We exchanged a few emails and she informed me that four tickets would be at "will call." We couldn't have been more excited. We bring my son and his twin sister to all kinds of concerts, but finally, there would be a show that was all about him!

We kept showing my son pictures of JT in the weeks and days leading up to the concert without knowing if he understood where we were going. We hadn't been to the Lake Tahoe venue before, and we didn't know where our seating was until we got there. When we finally arrived and saw the venue and all the JT signs, he understood what was about to happen. Figuring we'd be up in the bleachers, we got in line to get our tickets. They were not there. *Oh no.* Panic started to creep in when the lady asked me who told me our tickets would be at will call. I told her it was JT's personal assistant. She said, "Oh! You're in 'with the band' tickets."

The woman handed us our tickets and showed us a seating chart. We were center stage, row 8, and on an aisle. It was perfect! Aisle seating gives my son a bit more elbow room so he's not feeling crowded or overwhelmed. We couldn't have been more grateful or thrilled—it was a true blessing.

When James took the stage, the excitement in my son's eyes was as if he were visiting Disneyland for the first time. He smiled ear-to-ear the entire night. He sang, he danced, and he was beaming. My heart was full.

During intermission both my kids got autographs and pictures. It was truly a magical night, a night I will never forget—the night my boy got to meet one of his music heroes. I'll be forever grateful.

∿

Jon Reynolds – Reseda, CA

I became a fan of James Taylor's music in 1985 when I first heard "Your Smiling Face." I was 11 years old. I had no idea at the time how meaningful this song would be for me much later in my life.

The first time I met James was in 1998, at a night club in Studio City, California, where I went to see a solo show by Arnold McCuller. Sitting at the club, I looked out the window and saw JT standing on the sidewalk. I was excited, so I ran outside to ask for an autograph and photo. JT graciously obliged. He then came in to watch

Arnold's show. Since then, I've taken every opportunity I can to meet him.

In August the same year, JT performed at the Universal Amphitheater. After my being persistent for three nights in a row, the manager of the theater finally let me backstage. I was able to meet his backup singers, Valerie Carter and Kate Markowitz, along with James' daughter, Sally. We posed for a picture together.

When I saw JT at Wilshire Theater in Beverly Hills, he had driven himself to the venue, so it was super easy to meet him. I asked him if I could sing a song with him, and of course he said "No." I said to myself that I just had to find a way to get him to say "Yes!"

In November 2007, I found out at the last minute that JT was doing a DVD signing in Santa Monica at Barnes and Noble, so I booked it down to meet him. When I met him at the signing table, I asked if he would sing "Happy Birthday" with me for a friend. He said, "Sure!" I was in shock. The people in line at the book signing cheered!

The next opportunity I got was on my birthday in July of 2008. JT was playing at the Greek Theater in Los Angeles. I went down early, and his drummer, Steve Gadd, helped me get an autograph. Later that year in November, JT played a series of shows at the Troubadour in Los Angeles with Carole King for their fiftieth anniversary celebration, and I went almost every night.

Next, JT was on Jay Leno's "last" episode of "The Tonight Show," on May 29th, 2009. He had his driver stop the car so he could sign autographs. I asked him again if he would sing "Happy Birthday" for a (different) friend with me, and he did—again!

I've been able to sing with James Taylor twice. A dream come true—twice!

When JT was on "Jimmy Kimmel Live" in 2015, I made it to the studio just in time. James came over and signed an autograph for me, and I told him that I had a story to share.

In 2007, I had seen my future wife in a dream: She would have a tattoo on her collarbone that said "Lovely." That dream came to fruition in 2014, when I met my wife Danyell, who has the same tattoo! And then I realized that the first JT song I heard was also about a *lovely lady* and I realized, "Oh my God! This girl was mentioned to me way back when I was eleven years old when I first heard the song "Your Smiling Face!"

James said in response, "You've got something special going on there. What are your names?" He signed a photo to both of us.

James played on an outdoor stage for the show, so I heard him rehearse the songs. In rehearsal, he didn't sing "Your Smiling Face," but for the show, he did.

After the show, James came to the front of the stage to sign more autographs. I thanked him for singing "Your Smiling Face," and he replied, "You're welcome! I know how much that song means to you."

I have twenty-four autographed items of JT memorabilia, including tickets, t-shirts, and CDs, and I hope to continue my collection as the years go on!

Thank you, James.

Mark Straub – Rochester, NY

My connection with the power of James Taylor's words grew stronger after my daughter's birth at Highland Hospital in Rochester, New York, and has continued to grow every day since.

Our daughter was due to be born on March 9. She didn't arrive on time. Five days later, a decision was made to admit my wife, Becky, to the hospital. As first-time parents, we were excited, nervous, and a bit scared. We had no idea what was about to happen.

Three days later, the doctors started to seem concerned and a new team joined us. Only one person remained constant: a per diem nurse, Therese, who was also a family friend. Therese was calm and collected, but I could tell that her tone changed with the doctor. Things needed to happen fast; both mother and baby were stressed.

Finally, on St. Patrick's Day, our daughter, Ella, came into the world. The delivery was difficult—incredibly hard on Becky, and harder still on our baby.

I was worried. "Is something wrong?" I asked.

A doctor told me to stand back, as I would not be able to cut the umbilical cord. Beck was exhausted, beat up, and could tell that Ella was in trouble. Nurses were discussing APGAR scores: "extremely low, weak, grey, no cry." I was standing to the side, close to Becky, trying to determine what to do. A nurse called to me, "Come with us, Dad." I looked at my wife, and the doctors and nurses working on her. Becky managed a smile to assure me that she would be fine, and that it was OK for me to go.

Out of the room, I passed by Ella's aunt and grandparents waiting in the wings with worried looks. I followed the nurse and my daughter, no cry yet, on her fast ride in a basinet on wheels to a windowless room filled with the hum of lighting and medical machines. She was connected to monitors, a beep here and there. I was a frozen man standing over our newborn. A nurse came to my side and said, "She knows you; she knows your voice. Sing to her, whatever song you know all the words to. It will help her."

I started to sing "Your Smiling Face."

"I love that song," the nurse said. "Keep it up, Dad. Your little girl is going to grow up strong and smart," she told me as I continued to sing.

Finally, a soft cry emerged.

I was eye-to-eye with my little girl, giving kisses on her forehead, shoulders, and hands, singing James' words, and even attempting the falsetto: "La la la la la la la la la la la …"

James Taylor's "Your Smiling Face" remains my all-time favorite JT song. I remember watching the WGBH live video version long before our daughter joined us. The guitar, bass, drums, keys, tempo and succinct lyrics lift you up, as does James' excitement, and that grimace when he performs the extra verse as he slings his guitar to the side.

That grimace—Ella has one, too, and it's beautiful.

The grit James has drawn upon to lift himself up and create music for all of us to enjoy—Ella has that grit, too.

In live performances, JT spins to see his musicians—the late and great ones, the current all-stars. Likewise, Ella has a team that she is a part of, our family. My wife and I, her two sisters, and her brother all know that "Your Smiling Face" is more than a two minute, 46 second track. It is about happiness, life, and love. It's her song.

Since Ella was a baby, that song is played frequently at home and in the car, but when we hear it in a grocery store or a restaurant, it comes to life in its own way. We sing, we dance, and we smile. I imagine, one day, at her wedding, it will be the song for our father-daughter dance. And when Ella's children come into the world, my hope is that it will be the first song they hear, too, and we all will continue to share the connection to James Taylor for generations to come.

CHAPTER 40

You've Got A Friend

Leslie Bines – Manhasset, NY

I fell in love with James Taylor at Tanglewood in 1970 when I was 10 years old attending a sleepaway camp in the beautiful Berkshires. I heard his magical voice, and I was forever hooked.

How do you measure a year? By minutes—525,600—or by seconds? By daylight, sunsets, laughter, or strife? The past forty-one years in my life could have been measured by unbearable ups and downs, and if it were not for James Taylor, I don't know how I would have gotten through them. His music is the very thing that runs through my soul. I have fought unbeatable foes, and I thank God every day for James. He is the soundtrack of my life, and I look forward every year to seeing him in concert.

On JT's DVD *Live at the Beacon Theater* from 1998, I am the one handing him a bouquet of flowers after he

sings "You've Got A Friend." Ever since that first time, I give him flowers at every concert I attend.

I often say, "I eat, breathe and sleep James Taylor." He has been a part of everything in my life: my adolescence, my wedding, the birth of my children, and my father's funeral. I dedicated four James Taylor songs at my father's unveiling ceremony, a Jewish ritual when the tombstone is placed on a grave.

To this day, I live by his lyric, "The secret of life is enjoying the passage of time." I am thankful my three grown children love and appreciate him, too. I even named my son "Taylor" after James.

I have so many *golden moments*, and I am forever grateful for my life with James Taylor.

You've got a friend for life in me, James.

Angela Elliot-Johnson - Kingsford, MI

"Nice to meet you," said James Taylor.

"Nice to meet you as well," I said, welling up with tears. He reached out to give me a hug.

It's hard to put into words how much this encounter meant to me. I have been listening to James Taylor's music since I was a very young girl. His music was a constant in my life, and still is to this day. My late father was a hippie from the 1970s and a huge fan of James Taylor. He would always play JT records on his turntable with the volume booming. Not only did he resemble James in his appearance—tall, handsome, and thin—but he also had a similar personality, at least as far as what I perceive James to have. Dad was shy, quiet, reflective, deep, artistic, and one with nature. I spent many hours alongside my father, memorizing James Taylor's profound lyrics.

When my wedding day came, it was obvious to me that I needed a JT song for my father/daughter dance. We chose "You've Got A Friend."

About eighteen years ago, James Taylor performed in Green Bay, Wisconsin, to promote his *October Road* album. My dad and I went to the concert together, and it was amazing. He shared with me at that concert that his favorite song was "Belfast To Boston." That song will always remain precious to me for that reason.

My dad passed away suddenly of a brain aneurism on May 26, 2004, just after his fiftieth birthday. My mom and I were devastated, and our lives changed forever. When the time came to choose his headstone, we decided to inscribe it with the lyrics from "You've Got A Friend." I've spent many days at the cemetery with Dad, playing some of our favorite songs.

A few years after losing my dad, my mom and I found out that JT was going to perform another concert in Green Bay. We attended with heavy hearts, yet with so much excitement. I took a chance and asked an usher how it might be possible to meet James. She stealthily gave us directions to the back of the arena, where his tour bus was parked. We waited in the cold fall air for what seemed like forever. And then, just like that, James appeared in front of us.

I was awestruck. He gave me a hug and posed for a photo with me. I mustered up enough courage to tell him that I have been a lifelong fan, and that his lyrics are engraved on my father's headstone. He was so kind and gracious to listen to me gush on and on.

It was a full circle moment in my life that I will never forget. I know there was one incredible angel in heaven who shared that once-in-a lifetime moment with me that night.

Thank you, James, for being in my father's life, and mine.

Joel Goodin – Middlesboro, KY

I was raised on the mellower side of rock and roll, listening to the great harmonies of CSNY, Simon & Garfunkel, Joni Mitchell, Joan Baez, and of course, James Taylor. The first time I saw James Taylor in concert, he was on stage singing "You've Got A Friend" with Carole King accompanying him on piano. I fell in love with his music instantly. I ran out and bought all his albums I could find: *The Original Flying Machine, Sweet Baby James, Mud Slide Slim, One Man Dog.*

I was elated when, in 1974 or 1975, while attending Eastern Kentucky University in Richmond, Kentucky, I was working as a member of the student concert crew, hauling musical equipment and such for the performers, and James came to perform! After we got the stage set up, the crew and the band members were invited to a catered dinner. I made sure I sat right across from James, excited for my opportunity to have a conversation with this artist I so deeply admired. But I was so nervous that I just sat there, frozen. No words came out! I finally had a chance to speak with this man that I had loved for so many years and I couldn't get anything to come out!

Still, to this day, he is my favorite artist. Soothing and effortlessly performed, James Taylor's music takes me to a different place and time, and I am so grateful I discovered him so many years ago.

~

Lynda Schanne - Stratford, NJ

Wherever I am, when the song "You've Got A Friend" comes on the radio, everyone knows not to say a word to me until it's over.

When I married my husband, John, in 1978, it was the song for our first dance. When my sister-in-law, who took me to my first JT concert in 1979, passed away, we played it at her funeral.

The first time I heard James Taylor I was 13 years old, in the summer of 1971. I was visiting my cousins in Maine, hanging around the arcade when "You've Got A Friend" came on the jukebox. I fell in love with James Taylor instantly.

"You've Got A Friend" is still my hands-down favorite to this day, nearly fifty years later.

For years, when my mom heard that song come on, she would call my phone and let it play over my voicemail for a minute or two, just to let me know she was thinking about me. I remember going to the JT / Carole King Troubadour Reunion tour in 2010, when they sang "You've Got A Friend" together. I called my mom and let her listen on my phone while they sang; it was one of the most precious memories I have. I also ran up to the stage and had JT sign my *Mud Slide Slim* album cover. My knees were weak, and I thought I was going to faint. I'm not sure how I did it, but I did and watched in awe as he got closer and closer to me. It was finally my turn and I went totally white I am sure. I somehow mustered up the courage to tell him how much I loved him, and then the rest is a blur. I do remember walking back to my seat and holding that album so tight and thinking to myself, *I can't believe I just did that, got close to him, actually said something to him.* It is one of my most cherished moments ever.

My mom passed away in 2014. Aside from missing literally everything about her, there are two things I miss the most: one is not getting a wakeup call from her on my birthday every year, and the other is those surprise JT voicemails.

Recently I started to teach my 6-year-old granddaughter how to sing and play "You've Got A Friend" on piano and guitar. When she sings it to me, my heart melts. That song has been with me for so many years, it's simply a piece of who I am.

James Taylor, you've got a friend in me.

☙

Regina Vater - São Paulo, Brazil

The first time I lived in New York, I made friends with one of the most important Brazilian artists of the last century. His name was Hélio Oiticica. At that time, Oiticica was just a myth; only after his early death did the market recognize him as genius. Today his works are displayed in museums internationally.

Because he lived in an unsafe part of Manhattan, most of our conversations took place over the telephone. We spent hours talking about everything from highbrow subjects to mundane things like recipes for cakes and cookies. I learned a lot about philosophy, poetry, and music from him. A few days before I returned to Brazil, he invited me to visit him. Before I left his loft that afternoon, he gave me James Taylor's record, "You've Got A Friend," with a sweet dedication. After I settled down in São Paulo, I bought a record player to listen to Oiticica's gift and immediately fell in love with James Taylor. I couldn't stop listening to him. After that special gift I started to collect James Taylor's records.

In the 1980s, I fell in love with an American artist I met at one of my shows and decided to return to New York. To raise some money for the move, I held a garage sale of all my things, including

188

my record collection and record player. I couldn't sell that special record of James Taylor's, which had a cherished meaning for me, representing Oiticicas's friendship. But I was also afraid to bring it with me to New York, because I feared I could lose it just as I'd lost so many other things during my travels and moving abroad.

I decided to give it to a Brazilian friend. That was a heartbreaking decision, and one I regret to this day. I am afraid to ask my friend if he still has my James Taylor record!

Every time that I hear James Taylor's music, I feel the presence of my late friend Hélio Oiticica. Because of this special memory, I have to say that James Taylor is the most magical American musician; his music is so simple and heart touching and brings back so many memories of my wonderful friend.

~⊸

Lori Zieman – Rochester Hills, MI

The gentleness of James Taylor's voice calms my being. When I am blue, it soothes me. When I am filled with worry and anxiety, his music calms me. When I am happy, I sing along to his songs. Whatever the mood, I feel at peace listening to James Taylor. His music has indeed touched my soul.

Many years back, in my hometown of Rochester Hills, Michigan, I used to love to climb up on the flat part of my roof on a warm summer evening with a glass of wine in my hand and listen to "Up On The Roof." I would play the song over and over, until my wine was gone. It was so soothing.

About twenty-three years ago, God blessed me with my second child. In the middle of the night, when I would wake up to the cry of my sweet little baby—who just happened to be named James (*I wonder why?*)—I would hold him in my arms and rock-a-bye *my* Sweet Baby James until he would fall back asleep. This was soothing to me, too.

Three years later, I found myself faced with a most difficult time in my life, and I was forced to end my marriage. I embarked on a new chapter in my life with my two young sons. I wanted to leave all the lies, abuse, and deception behind me, yet I felt so very lost and alone. Aware of my pain, my dear friend and her wonderful husband took me to the Pine Knob Music Theater in Clarkston, Michigan, to see James Taylor. I had seen him many times before, but this time was different—I was front row and center stage!

James was amazing, as usual. During my ultimate favorite song, "You've Got A Friend," I began to weep. As James Taylor reached his hand out to mine, I deeply sensed he could feel my pain. He was so comforting and uplifting to my broken spirit.

Thank you, James. You've got a friend in me.

EPILOGUE

The Secret O' Life

My husband picks up his guitar, carries a chair to the middle of the backyard and sits down. Instinctively, the party guests gather around him.

"I'd like to dedicate this song to my wife," he says. "Today, on her fiftieth birthday."

My husband, Osvaldo, is a classical guitarist, but when he begins finger picking in a manner so unlike his usual style, I immediately recognize the intro, although I've never heard him play this song in the twenty-five years we've been married. With his sweet South American accent, he starts to sing my all time favorite James Taylor song: "The Secret O' Life."

I look around at the group of people gathered at this party and I smile from deep within. Tables are decorated with pictures and albums of James Taylor, alongside photos of people from my past, many of whom are here today: my ex-husband; my oldest childhood friends; my college roommate; and a number of my *BFGF* (big fat Greek family) including my mother, my sisters, their spouses, kids and grandkids,

and several aunts, cousins and friends. And of course, my three children softly sing along, knowing all the words.

Everyone here knows they are witnessing a special moment, although most do not know how profound it is for me.

I think about a time, more than twenty years ago, when Osvaldo and I were newlyweds. We had decided to spend Thanksgiving weekend with our collective family, brothers and sisters, spouses and kids, and we all pitched in to rent a cozy cottage in Big Bear, California. While the children were playing board games, the adults gathered around the fireplace, drinking wine and eating cheese and crackers. My mother, always the one to spark group conversation, suggested we play a game.

"Question and Answer," she said.

"You mean Truth or Dare?" my brother-in-law said, laughing.

"Sort of," she said. "But let's just stick to truth. Each one of us will ask a meaningful question to the group, and then we'll share answers."

She handed each of us a scrap of paper and a pencil. "But you have to write down your answer before we share," she instructed. "That way no one in the group can influence your response, OK?"

We all nodded in agreement.

I'll start," she said. "My first question is this: If you had only one day left to live, who would you want to spend it with?"

"Does the person have to be alive?" my sister asked.

"Nope," Mom said. "It can be anyone, dead or alive. Anyone at all."

The ten of us contemplated, giggled, closed our eyes, and then finally scribbled down answers. When we were all finished, my mother said, "OK, let's go around the circle and read our answers. Who wants to start?"

My sister Pam and her husband, David, were seated to my left. Pam and Dave had been together since high school, married for thirteen years, and had a daughter and son together. Dave was the first to answer.

"Pam," he said confidently. "I wouldn't want to spend my last day with anyone else besides my wife." He leaned over and gave her a kiss on the cheek.

Pam quickly piped up, unfolding her paper. "Well that's good, because my last day would be with you, Dave," she said, taking hold of his hand.

"Oh, that's beautiful," my mother responded. "What about you, Jen?" she asked my younger sister.

Jennifer unfolded her slip of paper, "Well, this is interesting, she said. "I chose Tom." She was referring to her husband of ten years, with whom she shared a son and daughter.

Tom quickly unfolded his paper and showed it to the group, "Jen!" he announced proudly, as he put his arm around her and gave her a squeeze.

Osvaldo's brother and his wife followed suit, each answering their last day would be spent with each other.

My mother smiled broadly, while I started to sweat, just slightly, noticing the emerging theme.

"And you, Osvaldo?" My mother asked. Osvaldo and I had met just a little over a year earlier and were now married for a whopping two months. This was his first marriage, my second, and I had a 7-year-old daughter. Osvaldo had immigrated to the United States six years prior from Uruguay, and was new to many of our customs, like Thanksgiving, or playing Truth or Dare. But somehow, even he caught on to the theme and played it perfectly.

"Of course, it is Rebecca," he announced, opening his slip of paper for everyone to see. "The love of my life."

"Aww," the group responded in unison. Osvaldo wrapped his arms around me and planted a sweet kiss on my cheek.

Now it was my turn. I looked up at the group of faces waiting eagerly for me to unfold my scrap of paper. I looked at my new husband and smiled.

"Go ahead," he said. "Answer the question. Who would you spend your last day with?"

I unfolded my paper, and quietly read: "James Taylor."

The group erupted in laughter. Osvaldo shook his head. "I should have known!"

"I'm just being honest," I said.

Osvaldo wasn't mad or jealous or even surprised at my response. And still to this day, twenty-five years and three kids later, my answer might still be the same. And it's not because I don't love or enjoy spending time with my husband, or my children, or anyone else in my life. It's because, quite simply, if it wasn't for James Taylor and his music, I believe I might not *be* alive today.

I was one lucky lady. Lucky to have emerged from the darkness of my early teenage years when a dangerous man claiming to be a spiritual teacher seduced me into his dark and damaging world. And luckier still that my ninth grade music teacher was a James Taylor fan, and when she played the song "Fire And Rain" to the class, something inside of me broke open and I realized I wasn't alone in the dark.

James Taylor revealed his pain and inner struggles in that song, and somehow it made me feel known, and even hopeful. He faced his furies, and that came out in his music. Listening to that song made me believe that I could do the same. The music and poetry of James Taylor gave me the strength to break away from the hell my life had become. He was my friend, my therapist, my guide. And as the years went on, I continued to count on him and his music to be beside me through the good times and bad.

And here I am now, on my fiftieth birthday, listening to my husband sing my favorite James Taylor song.

I gave him a heartfelt kiss. And then, completely impromptu, he begins to play another song, to which all our guests know the words and sing along: "You've Got A Friend."

Here's to my friend.
Here's to the secret of life.
My life with James Taylor.

ACKNOWLEDGMENTS

First and foremost, I am filled with gratitude for James Taylor and his All-Star Band for sharing their lives with me and adoring fans all over the world. In particular, I want to thank Arnold McCuller for bringing my phone on stage during the last Tanglewood concert and filming the coolest upfront and personal video of "How Sweet It Is!" (You can check out the video on my Facebook page: *Life With James Taylor*). I also want to thank Andrea Zonn for her virtual "Storytime with Zonny" nights which have been incredibly healing throughout covid when we were unable to go to live events.

Thank you to my JTBFFs, those who have contributed to this book, and those cheering me on from the sidelines. Thank you to Kim Lifton for her friendship and unwavering support every step of the way, Leslie Bines for coining the term "JTBFF," and my BFGF (*big fat Greek family*) who have never, *ever*, called me a stalker (at least not to my face.)

A huge thank you to Jordan Cook who kept me organized throughout this entire process because my brain simply doesn't work the amazing way that hers does.

Finally, thank you to my husband Osvaldo who never complains when I say "Yes, we are going to ANOTHER James Taylor concert!" (And also never complained when I said, "Yes, we are driving four hours during a snowstorm to see James Taylor's theatrical debut in a community theater two days before Christmas!")

And my children: Nisha, Camila, and Oliver for listening to me sing and dance and tell stories about James Taylor throughout their entire lives … and never calling anyone "JT" except the one and only, James Vernon Taylor.

ABOUT THE AUTHOR

Rebecca Lyn Gold is an author, editor, and the founder of YogicWriting.com, a practice for writers of all levels to heal, reveal, and leave a legacy through writing life stories.

She is the author of *Till There Was You: An Adoption Expectancy Journal*, *A Wizard Called Woz: a biography of Stephen Wozniak*, *How To Write It Funny* with author/humorist Amy Koko, and *From Your Mat to Your Memoir: Creating a yogic writing practice to find and write your life stories.*

From the early 1970s when Rebecca first heard the song "Fire And Rain," James Taylor has been a source of inspiration and healing throughout her life.

Rebecca lives in Rhode Island with her husband, Osvaldo. They have three children, four grandchildren, and one sweet puppy, Brownie.

If you have a story you would like to share for an upcoming edition of "That's Why We're Here" contact Rebecca@LifeWithJamesTaylor.com